"Allen Hamlin writes on followership with an elevating language that imbues this form of relationship with service, grace, and individuality. A very welcome addition to the growing literature on followership."

—Ira Chaleff, author of *The Courageous Follower*

"*Embracing Followership* may be among the top 10 most fresh, provocatively insightful expressions of what kind of thinking can 'set the readers free' from mindless cultural expectations on us that we've unconsciously imbibed. If you are one of the multitudes who can't escape thinking you should be more of a leader, this book is for you. It marvelously clarifies the reality of how we are all both leaders and followers and are 'blessed' when we find ourselves 'at home' with that reality. I plan to distribute dozens of copies!"

—Greg Livingstone, founder, Frontiers

"*Embracing Followership* challenged and changed me—one of the rare books that can challenge your worldview and make you glad you read it. Allen manages to exalt followers without disparaging leaders, proving the unique value of each and providing practical steps to move us toward the mutually beneficial place of respect and value for the contributions of both."

—T. J. MacLeslie, minister, missionary, and
author of *Designed for Relationship*

"I love Allen's heart and the book God has grown out of who he is. He is right. We live in a 'leader-driven culture' where there is little focus on the spiritual integrity and dignity of 'followership.' Jesus called us to 'follow Him,' and the church is the strongest when together we follow Him and the design He has for us as His people. We are called to excel in followership. Well done, Allen, and thank you."

—Dr. Hal Habecker, founder, Finishing Well Ministries

"The genius of Allen's approach and treatment of this subject of "followership" is that each of us is a follower in some way in almost every aspect of our lives. This is a thoughtful exploration and consideration of what it means to excel as a follower, which is essential for all of us to enhance our friendships, our workplaces, our communities, and our faith. *Embracing Followership* should be required reading for those working in a group setting, since developing our followership abilities has a direct effect on improving our teams, our leaders, and our organizations."

—Duane E. Okamoto, senior attorney, Microsoft Corporation

EMBRACING FOLLOWERSHIP

How to Thrive in a Leader-Centric Culture

EMBRACING
FOLLOWERSHIP

How to Thrive in a Leader-Centric Culture

ALLEN HAMLIN JR.

KIRKDALEPRESS

Embracing Followership:
How to Thrive in a Leader-Centric Culture

Copyright 2016 Allen Hamlin Jr.

Kirkdale Press, 1313 Commercial St., Bellingham, WA 98225
KirkdalePress.com

Print ISBN 978-1-57799-632-3
Digital ISBN 978-1-57799-633-0

Kirkdale Editorial Team: Rebecca Brant, Lynnea Fraser, Joel Wilcox
Cover Design: Jon Deviny and Christine Gerhart
Back Cover Design: Brittany Schrock
Typesetting: ProjectLuz.com

Dedicated to the unknown crew who served on my flight
from Hong Kong to Thailand in October 2011.
Thank you for serving with excellence and creating space
for me to be inspired to write this book.

CONTENTS

INTRODUCTION

In 2011, while flying from Hong Kong to Thailand, I read a book called *A Vision of the Possible*. In it, the author makes a passing comment that there are numerous books about how to lead well, but what we really need is a book on how to be a good follower.[1]

With that single sentence, while soaring at 35,000 feet, everything snapped into focus for me: I would explore the topic of followership. For years, I have served among and alongside leaders at the highest level of our organization, and as result, I have read a lot of books about leadership. However, I've never felt like I was part of the target audience. Relatively few authors or leadership gurus are interested in making an investment in *followers*. I was often left wondering: "Where is the book for *me*?"

Surely, in this new category of followership, I would find the guidance I needed. A dozen books later, however, I still hadn't found what I was looking for: a work treating followership as its own endeavor, not as a style of leadership or a way to build a career, but as the pursuit of participation and contribution in its own right. A book that says followers need not be recast as leaders in order to be legitimate and valuable.

And that is the book I set out to write.

My intent in this book is to equip those in follower roles to understand, value, and execute those roles with excellence.

Whether we work in an office, sit in a classroom, serve on a committee, play on a team, or join in a congregation, we are followers whenever other people have titles, authority, and responsibility that include us within their sphere of oversight.

We are followers, and we call those above us leaders. If that label feels uncomfortable or demeaning to you, read on. Part of our journey will be to overcome the negative stereotypes attached to the word "follower"—even those we tend to believe ourselves.

This is not a book on leadership strategy or about *creating* good followers. It is an investigation into how to *be* a good follower. It is an encouragment to shift our perspective about our leaders and ourselves to one that enables us to contribute as followers with both contentment and excellence.

Many people view followership as a kind of purgatory, as the thing you endure before you get to move on to something greater and more profitable. But I certainly do not agree with this view, so I was encouraged when I discovered that it's not at all universal, as revealed in these words: "More people admit to me that they not only play the follower role but also prefer it."[2] So can we instead agree that, for some of us, being a follower is who we are? It's our role, our duty, our obligation, even our calling?

Are you, like me, concerned with being a good team player, and with using your gifts, talents, and abilities? Do you desire to make a positive impact and contribution to the many circles of association in which you are involved? Are you looking for the book that will encourage and accompany you as you invest in yourself and in your followership role?

I suspect that you picked up this book, in part, because you answered yes to the above. I believe that only a deeply internal drive can create the motivation for performing with excellence, finding satisfaction, and offering one's gifts and talents in pursuit of a larger purpose and for the betterment of others.

For me, that drive has been fueled by my Christian faith and the affirming community that has surrounded me in the form of coworkers and friends. As the anonymous author of *Embracing Obscurity*³ reminds me, I am significant, but not because of my fame (which is none), the admiration of others (which is limited), or my experience (more than some, less than others). Rather, my significance comes, in part, from the truth that I have an important role to fulfill and a vital contribution to make.

Developing this perspective has been a personal journey for me, and the language and acknowledgment of followership have been tools I've used to move forward in valuing who I am.

Throughout this book, you will see many quotations and references to the work of other authors. Hearing the perspectives—both positive and negative—of other followers has allowed me to engage with the follower role and clarify my own thinking. I invite you to do the same, as you question these ideas for yourself. I have found these words particularly inspiring in my pursuit: "A follower does not need credentials or recognition ... [He or she] only needs to show up and be there and, when appropriate, point the way for others who are traveling in the same direction."⁴ In that spirit, I offer you what I have discovered in hopes that you, too, might find—perhaps for the first time—the kind of encouragement, perspective, and direction that you've been looking for.

1

A PRIMER ON FOLLOWERSHIP

As followers, our foremost relationship is with our leaders, and so let us begin to shape our understanding of followership with a brief reflection on leadership.

We exert leadership in countless areas: We make decisions at home; we live by example as a member of a sports team; we wield influence within our social circle, and so on. This kind of leadership can occur within relatively loose relationship dynamics; we don't need to be the team captain to guide others.

But the type of leadership that provides a counterpart for followership, as we have defined it, is *formal* leadership: someone within a particular organization, association, or community who has been given authority for making decisions and overseeing a group. In Western cultures, that responsibility is often denoted by a title: director, chairperson, chief officer, principal, captain, manager, senior pastor, coach, and so on.

These formal leadership roles have been established to direct and guide other people, for whom such leaders are responsible; these others are followers. At its heart, followership is the complement to leadership. You can't have one without the other. This doesn't mean that followers are defined by what leaders are *not*. A follower is a leader's counterpart, not his or her opposite.

It's also important to note that many followers simultaneously have leadership roles. Like followership, leadership may be voluntary or compulsory. Leaders are elected, appointed, chosen, hired, or sometimes simply installed. I once discovered that I was responsible for leading a group when I came across my name printed in the organization's newsletter!

In fact, we can hold follower and leader roles at the same time in some of the very same contexts. For example, at work I currently have two levels of supervisors above me, but I also function as an area leader, overseeing five teams (and their leaders), who operate across three countries. In my church, someone else is the pastor ("vicar" as we say here in the U.K.), but I'm the leader of the monthly Bible study. Even in the publication of this

> "If each of us is a follower at some level, why not put my efforts into being the best follower rather than focusing on leadership?"
> (*Power of Followership*, 82)

book, I have (at least officially!) veto power over the editorial process, but I know that final authority for many decisions belongs to the graphic designer and marketing director.

So this is not an *us* (followers) versus *them* (leaders) pursuit; we may soon enough find ourselves bearing a leadership title, even if that is not our goal. To maintain a helpful, realistic perspective, we won't demonize leaders, nor will we pretend they don't exist.

Setting the Stage for Followership

The term "followership," as we're using it here, is a relatively new term, popularized in the early 1990s. However, with the more recent advent of Twitter and other social media, the notion of *following* has been redefined as something markedly different. Whereas Twitter followership can be merely an expression of appeal or the fruit of charisma, the kind of followership we're looking at is the reality of a relational dynamic that exists within any community that has one or more formal leaders.

When I mention the word "followership" to others with the definition we are using here, even those who have never heard it before instantly feel a sense of resonance with the idea—it expresses a reality they can easily relate to. There's a simple reason for this: In some sense, *we are all followers*. Whether we have a leadership title, or whether we are self-employed, unemployed, subcontracted, full-time students, homemakers, hobbyists, or pew-warmers, we all have someone who is over us—someone providing direction, accountability, decision-making, and representation. Even CEOs have board members, team captains have coaches, committee chairs report to constituents and general assemblies. As such, we all have experience with followership, even if we have not encountered or explored the concept.

Sometimes we are a follower by choice. We join a club, volunteer for a project, or accept a job. But sometimes we are a follower by obligation. For example, we are citizens of a particular nation, which gives us civic responsibilities. We may be required to participate in a class (anyone else ever been ordered to take a driving safety refresher course?). Or we may be called to take our turn for the neighborhood watch rotation.

Whether our followership is voluntary or unavoidable, we have similar opportunities and obligations. The degree to which we participate, the excellence we contribute, the attitude we experience (both within ourselves and from others) are all part of any followership experience.

Of course, following plays out in different ways. Our individual personalities, cultures, and organizations affect how we fulfill follower roles, and we will address these factors in the course of our exploration. But a more fundamental concern is our perspective on our own followership. We can be good followers or bad ones. Engaged or passive. Helpful or hindering.

Followership allows for a variety of styles and degrees of participation. It may mean doing little more than what you're told to do. It could even mean actively (or passively) resisting the tasks assigned to you. This is technically following, but it is not following well.

We are seeking *excellent* followership—our valuable contribution to a collective effort. This can range across a broad spectrum of involvement. You may be faithfully fulfilling your job description, responding to the requests made of you, and/or applying the best of your time, energy, talents, and resources to further a group's aims. You may in fact play an extremely vital role in the success of your association or workplace.

For example, a friend recently told me about one of his colleagues, Colin. Colin was a relatively low-level but long-serving member of an IT team at a sizeable British company. In a round of downsizing, Colin was laid off ("made redundant" as they say in the U.K.). Known to his immediate peers, but overlooked by the supervisors who made the layoffs, Colin had often gone far beyond his job description to organize information and attend to client details that kept the company operating smoothly and profitably.

Some months after his dismissal, a review of accounts uncovered more than £4 million in missing revenue! It turns out that Colin had developed software for processing client subscription renewals, and no one else was even thinking about them. With Colin gone, no one processed the renewals, and the company never got paid. Colin was a "linchpin" follower in this organization, albeit a highly undervalued and unappreciated one.

Think for a moment about your follower roles. Where are you formally participating in some group or organization under the direction, responsibility, or authority of someone in a formal leadership role? I encourage you to keep in mind one of those roles as you continue reading. You might select the role that you are already most passionate about, but you hope to move into a yet more fulfilling and exciting level of involvement. Maybe you would like to be a linchpin follower like Colin, though that doesn't need to be your goal in every realm of followership.

Perhaps you'll want to focus instead on the most discouraging of your follower roles—one in which you feel dissatisfied, disempowered, and in need of encouragement and a fresh perspective. The goal here may not be to become the key to your organization's success, but rather to take a few steps toward experiencing satisfaction and meaningful involvement.

Whichever role you hold in mind as you read, you will see that since much of the work to be done is within us—to shape our perspectives, enhance our motivations, engage in relationships, surmount challenges—the concepts we explore will fit your context. As we look into these ideas together, apply them to your unique circumstances and according to your individual style.

Following Our Calling

I think it's fair to say that our very *first* calling is to be followers. We are born into this world subject to the authority and provision of parents or caretakers. Most of us don't come into this life as rulers of our own little kingdoms, even if we are well into adolescence before we realize this!

As I bring my own Christian background to this journey, I notice Jesus Christ's first invitation was often, "Follow me." He didn't say, "Lead me" or "Follow me so that you can lead others" or even "Follow me and I'll reward you with leadership." He simply said, "Follow me." In fact, one of the founding fathers of the modern exploration of followership, Robert Kelley, notes that "major religions ... are fertile grounds for examining followership."[1] Indeed, his own considerations turn to Christianity and the example of Jesus and his disciples.[2]

> "An emphasis on followers is not a de-emphasis on leaders" (*Follower First*, 49).

For some people, an invitation to be a follower feels like a woeful calling to be ordinary and insignificant. As author Jim Smoke observes, "In the age of the sensational, the superb, and the extraordinary, who in their right mind wants to be ordinary? Ordinary is being *in* the line when everyone wants to be at the *head* of the line."[3] But we are all followers, and if we neglect to thoughtfully consider our followership, or fail to invest in helping others develop as followers, we only contribute to organizational dysfunction.

Many of our cultures are leader-centric; we have long looked at leaders as the predominant influence, believing that if we could just make the right investment in them, the trickle-down effect would be enough to guarantee good results. While there is some truth to that thought, either we haven't succeeded in sufficiently equipping leaders, or the trickle-down effect is less significant than we supposed.

Instead, we find ourselves with crises and dysfunction that are fundamentally issues of followership.[4] After all, followers are the largest proportion of any group; to ignore the individual and collective influence of followers is to virtually condemn our associations to disappointment and failure.

And that negligence is not only on the part of the "others" who should be investing in followers. We bear the most responsibility for our own growth, development, involvement, and attitude.

I once knew a small team that was experiencing some internal difficulty. The team members and team leader were clearly not on the same page. When the conflict peaked, a team member wrote a manifesto to the leader declaring, "My preferred leadership style is total and complete autonomy."

While this team didn't directly affect me, I felt outraged and astonished at this perspective. This person had agreed to join the team, only to announce that he was unwilling to serve under someone else's leadership.

Such a perspective highlights our deep need for understanding our role in creating an empowering group dynamic—one in which both leaders and followers are freed, encouraged, and valued. Only then can they each make their respective contributions.

We must also be mindful of engaging with the right posture and motivation. We must not expect others to tell us what we need to be. And we must not hold others—leaders or followers—responsible for our own deficiencies in perspective or participation.

We may have adopted patterns and attitudes that detract from a positive and profitable group experience, and it falls to us to sort through them—weeding out any that weaken our appreciation for our role or our leaders.

So how will we make this investment? And how will we encourage other followers to reach a new level of satisfaction and effectiveness?

We turn first to reshaping our own paradigms concerning followership as we address some of the misconceptions about what it means to be a follower.

Part 1

MISCONCEPTIONS AND REALITIES OF FOLLOWERSHIP

There are many strands of misconceptions about followership. These strands have been woven together in our lives, communities, and cultures—to the point that they almost guarantee no one would choose followership as an arena for personal growth.

Our task is to disentangle these strands from our perspectives about ourselves and other followers.[1] Each strand is composed of a variety of threads, and the particular combination of threads that have contributed to your perspective may differ from those that have woven themselves into someone else's.

But for the sake of simplicity, I will focus on the three strands that have most significantly affected our thinking and practice: (1) followers' thoughts about followership (i.e., themselves), (2) leaders' thoughts about followership, and (3) followers' thoughts about leadership. These perspectives have shaped our systems, expectations, and relationships in ways that have often led us to de-emphasize the importance of cultivating excellence among followers.

The primary responsibility for participation and the pursuit of excellence lies with us, the followers. We are not simply victims of the world system or the leadership juggernaut that is so prevalent around us—we are a party to it. Therefore, we both begin and end this section by examining the strands of thought that originate within ourselves as followers.

2

FOLLOWERSHIP
ACCORDING TO FOLLOWERS

As a follower, you've likely heard slogans or mantras that paint a picture of what a right and valuable life looks like. Have you internalized these ideas and allowed them to become defining factors in how you see yourself? If so, then they have shaped your motivations and contentment—or your lack of motivation and sense of discontent. In what ways do these ideas affect your feelings about your current position, title, or involvement?

Many of us sat through graduation speeches that rang out, "You are the leaders of the next generation!" Most of us have been told "everyone is a leader," or perhaps even more specifically that "all wives/husbands/athletes/citizens/Christians/nurses[1]/managers/visionaries/teachers are leaders."

Although there may be some layers of truth in these slogans, for me they primarily served to create an internal sense of what I *wasn't* and what I must *become*. They set an expectation—one that may have been external initially, but that I quickly adopted as my own—for what my contribution, role, and life should be.

These expectations naturally led to comparison. I evaluated myself against those who clearly were leaders, noting which of their qualities I lacked or which of my own qualities seemed unfitting for someone predestined to be a leader. For a time, I struggled vainly to assert that I *was* a leader and should be acknowledged as such, though my title, role, and contribution were to the contrary. In search of an internal sense of value, I struggled to find a way to consider myself a legitimate member of the leadership class so esteemed by my culture.

> "No one is a failure or less important because he or she is deemed a follower"
>
> (*Follower First*, 21).

My own thoughts about followership were keeping me from following with excellence. And I've since discovered that I'm not alone in this. Here are four significant threads of misconceptions that we followers have about ourselves—ones I personally had to identify and replace with realities before I was free to truly follow with excellence.

Misconception: Leadership Is the Goal of Followership

The first misconception I developed was that I must make leadership my personal goal and ultimate aim—with the unspoken corollary that being a *mere* follower is not good enough.

To be a person of passion, ambition, enthusiasm, concern, influence, and excellence, I thought I needed to attain a leadership role. Once I had achieved a title, I would know that I had sufficient skill, experience, wisdom, and intelligence to make an impact. Until then, everything about me was suspect. Sure, we all have to start somewhere, but if I remained a follower for too long, people would raise serious questions about my value and abilities.

I believed leadership should not only be my primary goal, but also my standard of personal evaluation. I assessed my worth based on how close I was to a leadership position in light of how long I had been affiliated with a particular team or group.

Not that my boss would evaluate me this way, but my internal self-regard was tied to whether I was on the leadership track.

Misconception: I'm a Follower Because I'm a Coward

Leadership is strenuous work by all appearances: Leaders endure significant stress, make difficult decisions, engage in confrontations, and receive blame. But I began to wonder if by staying contentedly in my follower role, I was actually escaping or avoiding hard work. If I stay in the background, away from the front lines, I protect myself, escape injury, and keep my uniform nice and clean. Does that make me—whether by nature or personality—a coward who is fit only for a follower role?

Misconception: Followers Have No Authority or Influence

I have my own tasks and projects as a follower, but ultimately I have no authority, right? And without authority, do I lack influence as well? I may be able to prompt action with my emails or stir up problems through my negligence—but the real players are the ones with authority and influence.

If I'm content in my role as a follower, am I setting aside any real possibility to positively affect and shape the organization and people around me? As author Omokhai Imoukhuede notes, "few people associate followership with influence,"[2] and this perspective is found among followers just as often as it is among leaders.

Misconception: Followership Lacks Honor and Dignity

We all have to admit things to ourselves. We have to stand in front of the mirror and confront—and accept, to some extent—who we are. But would I feel content to know my gravestone preserves the memory that I "followed well"? Can I phone Mom and tell her that, yes, I am still in relatively the same position as I was eight years ago? My own experience leads me to agree with this statement: "We don't have a lot of people who know how to follow and feel significant."[3]

Many followers suffer from a sense of shame. Admitting that we are a volunteer and not the coordinator, that we are a constituent and not a decision-maker, that we are the assistant and not the executive (though perhaps the "executive assistant") can serve as a point of humiliation, of feeling not quite good enough. Uttering the words is akin to affirming defeat, placing a stamp of authenticity on others' suspicions that we are somewhat mediocre. We may have a slot on the roster, a position in the ranks, a chair in the room, but we aren't the captain, the commander, or the chairperson.

~~Misconception: Leadership Is the Goal of Followership~~

Reality: Followership Is Intrinsically Valuable

What truth stands against the misconstrued notion that I *must* be oriented toward attaining a leadership role? To begin with, I realized that while some societies may choose to elevate leaders to near heroic status, in the end, *leaders are just people*. Although much of Western cultural mythology tends to ascribe a legendary status to leaders because they "perform remarkable feats,"[4] followers are the essential supporting actors, without whom a scene is lifeless. Who wants to watch a lone actor on the big screen without others to play against, to fill in the details, to provide a backstory, and to establish a real, vibrant ensemble with which to create a powerful, artistic expression for reaching a wider audience?

Leaders may have characteristics, skills, and experience that I don't have, but then I, too, have qualities they lack. Whether considering education, previous employment outside of my current field, or administrative talent, I have come to see that everyone has a unique set of gifts, abilities, and experiences that can contribute to the group's projects and purpose.

Sometimes people's qualities are best employed in a position that requires taking responsibility for others and representing the corporation, organization, or community. I have found that my contributions don't necessarily benefit from such a platform, and they certainly don't require it. Instead, I have worked to shape my contentedness through the concept of "enoughness."[5] I want to make use of my skills and to engage in work that reflects my values and passions. I desire to serve, and my position gives me the opportunity to do so; what need do I have for a title?

~~Misconception: I'm a Follower Because I'm a Coward~~

Reality: Being an Excellent Follower Takes Courage

Only recently have I begun to oppose this myth about cowardice in my own life. At times I have had to push myself to speak up and act with courage.[6] I've had to make decisions about what is ethical and determine how to communicate while being sensitive of others. Being a follower certainly doesn't exempt us from hard work or difficult decisions.

Ira Chaleff's book *The Courageous Follower* addresses the inherent need, role, and responsibility of followers to act with bravery—amid risk—as they successfully fulfill their role. He notes, "Follower is not a term of weakness but the condition that permits leadership to exist and gives it strength."[7] Cowardice and weakness aren't inherent to followers—action and engagement are.

~~Misconception: Followers Have No Authority or Influence~~

Reality: Followers Can Exert Real Influence

As children, we all learned that despite having absolutely no authority over our parents, we could certainly exert plenty of influence. Our whining, stubbornness, and demands all served as weapons of manipulation to produce our desired outcomes. But these are examples of self-serving, short-term, and ultimately negative manifestations of influence. Is it possible that followers can contribute to a more positive outcome, even without having ultimate authority?

Even from a young age, we receive significant conditioning about the notion of leadership. While we are children at home and students in a classroom, "others are held responsible for our behavior, but we are not held responsible for theirs."[8] My teachers were charged with overseeing my actions, achievement, and welfare, and I was not at all responsible for their effectiveness and well-being.

> "The society in which I live, both secular and sacred, urges me upward to the next rung .... The problem is ... there is always another rung above. And soon the endless rungs become the only thing by which we measure ourselves" (*Whatever Happened to Ordinary Christians?*, 15).

The norm is that influence, authority, and responsibility flow downward, not upward. Such a perspective can actually lead us followers to overlook opportunities to exert influence and take personal responsibility, sometimes with disastrous results.[9] At the very least, our early experiences serve to instill in us the idea that we cannot and should not expect to have much influence until we have succeeded in attaining authority.

But I have evidence to the contrary. Having been with the same organization for a number of years, I have had multiple opportunities for involvement, and I've worked with people in diverse departments. I smile when it occasionally happens that someone sends me a document that is clearly based on my own earlier work. Sure, it has been adapted and customized along the way, but it has my fingerprints all over it—even though I may be the only one who sees them. My contribution has been used and recycled over the years. It has provided a platform for other projects and outlived its original intent. It has had an influence and affect, yet it was written at a time when I had no authority.

Perhaps part of this myth stems from confusing influence with recognition. We commonly seek to measure the results of our endeavors, and it's easy to see our influence when we receive recognition for it. If people know that we initiated, dreamed up, or carried out a particular project, then we've clearly made an impact.

We tend to think that since the names of an organization's followers tend to be less known than the names of its leaders, we are not likely to have much influence. People who have authority are necessarily known. After all, others must seek them out to get permission, resources, and access. But if no one ever seeks me out, if no one *needs* to come to me, if few know my name, how can I have influence?

In truth, I may have a great deal of influence but little recognition. And I can have influence even though I may not have authority. I can leave my fingerprints on every task, project, conversation, and relationship in which I participate. I may never have my name "in lights," and my influence may be hard to track or see on my résumé, but it is real. (Stay tuned for more about avenues for influence in Chapters 5 and 6.)

~~Misconception: Followership Lacks Honor and Dignity~~

Reality: Followers Are Noble and Worthy of Respect

The ancient world offers us a powerful corrective to the mistaken notion that followership lacks honor.[10] Think about Lancelot, Galahad, Bedivere, Percival, and Gawain. You may recognize these as the names of some of King Arthur's Knights of the Round Table, the medieval hallmark of honorable service. For these men, the call to follow King Arthur, to serve him and participate in his quests, was no mark of humiliation. Rather, being associated with—and in service to—this leader was the height of employee status in Europe at that time.

More than a thousand years earlier, Jesus Christ provided a similar opportunity when he invited 12 unknowns to be his disciples—his closest students, companions, and friends. "In the biblical culture it was a privilege to be asked to follow. All of those whom Jesus called were rejects who were not called to follow a rabbi ... Jesus gave them dignity by asking them to follow him."[11]

People who would otherwise have disappeared into history as nameless fishermen and tax collectors, instead became pillars of one of the world's great religions, through whom the lives of millions of people have been changed. Even if they did not experience the fullness of this honor in their own lifetimes—they were mocked and ridiculed even as Jesus was—we can learn from their experience that the follower role is not inherently one to be ashamed of.

Shame often derives from our understanding of external expectations. Whether we look to cultural values, family pressures, or membership qualifications, we find influences that define what is considered excellent and honorable. We, like others, make assumptions about which achievements are exceptional and which are expected, which involvements are treasured and which are merely accepted. In the face of these forces, to announce with any degree of pride, contentment, or enthusiasm that we are followers can be a most daunting act.

Here again, the temptation is for us to internalize and succumb to the prevailing winds of the environment around us. This is not to say that we can ignore all external expectations (we'll talk more about that in Chapter 9), but we must resist the personal value judgment that can arise when we allow stereotypes and norms to shape our self-perceptions, leading us to feel less than successful, important, valuable, honorable, or significant.

3

FOLLOWERSHIP
ACCORDING TO LEADERS

We have said that primary responsibility for our followership lies with us, but the simple reality is that the words and perspectives of those with authority have a significant effect on the culture and on those in follower roles. Leaders tend to be the dominant influencers in both organizations and society.

And while we bear responsibility for the degree to which we adopt unhealthy perspectives and allow them to prevent us from following with excellence, the regard that others have for followers is a profoundly significant influence in its own right. In some cases, we may have been overlooked, dismissed, or disregarded because of the perspectives held by those with power, position, and authority. It is worthwhile for us to identify some of these additional misconceptions so we can correct them— not just in our words but through the quality and character of our contribution.

While this chapter is entitled "Followership According to Leaders," it would be unfair to say that all leaders subscribe to the following misconceptions. In some cases, these misconceptions are more a result of broad cultural values than the actions or words of any single authority figure. Again, I'll be careful here to avoid the notion of an "us versus them" dynamic between followers and leaders; we have no need to believe we are victims of others' misconceptions.

Misconception: Followers Are Lemmings

If you were born in the early 1980s (or have children that age), you may remember a popular computer game called "Lemmings." In the game, the player had a number of creatures—small rodents infamously (and incorrectly) known for charging off of cliffs in stupefying acts of mass suicide—marching mindlessly across the screen. Play involved navigating the lemmings around certain obstacles to save them from violent death. Perhaps not surprisingly, the phrase "you're such a lemming" came to mean that you are a mindless follower, likely to fail in your endeavors ... unless someone else comes along to provide you with vision and direction—and perhaps even to take control of your very actions—in order to redeem your existence and turn your life toward some bit of achievement.

> "There exists the unspoken assumption that leaders have more to give than others, and that those who 'follow' need us more than we need them"
>
> (*I Am a Follower*, 175).

The qualities of vision and drive typically help define leadership, not followership. We tend to think leaders are the ones who can paint a compelling picture of the future and motivate others to get on board with making that vision a reality. We assume that those in leadership roles got there because they are persuasive and driven.

In contrast, we often assume followers are non-visionaries who lack sufficient drive or initiative to make things happen. Followers wait to be told what to do—imagine armies of ants or regiments of robots programmed to execute a single task.

Misconception: Followers Are Unqualified to Be Leaders

Some people claim that followers are unsuited for leadership, and I have seen this quality judgment play out in a number of ways. One notable trend is the middle ground we've created between leaders and followers. We use labels like "leader-in-training" and "emerging leader" to stratify the ranks of followers into those whose natural ability should be groomed for future use—to essentially identify where resources should be invested for the optimum return. I have not yet come across the terms "preeminent follower" or "followership role-model" to signify similar quality contributions and potential.

Misconception: Being a Follower Is the Polar Opposite of Being a Leader

The myth that followers can be characterized as the exact opposite of leaders is a common misconception even among those who typically uphold the value of followers and advocate for follower roles: "I define followers broadly, as 'unleaders,' if you will. They are without particular power, without positions of authority, and without special influence."[1] If a leader is X, then a follower is not-X.

Although this may be true at times—as when the leader has ultimate decision-making responsibility, and a follower does not—this notion implies a value judgment against the follower role. When coupled with another observation—"there are certain unflattering implications connected with the word follower: conforming, docile, easily manipulated, weak, unable to succeed on one's own, or simply 'not the leader' "[2]—it is clear that the culture is moving away from acknowledging role differences and toward making a statement of worth by polarizing leader and follower roles.

Misconception: Followers Only Follow to Get Ahead

If nothing disqualifies people from being leaders, why wouldn't everyone ultimately want to be a leader? If leadership were everyone's desire, follower roles would be nothing more than preparation for leadership—or a strategic play to usurp the leader when the timing was right.

Here we find ourselves at the opposite extreme from the misconceptions we've previously explored. Gone is the mindless, unmotivated lemming. Now we come across the conniving, manipulative follower who feigns quietude, subservience, and obedience only to bide his or her time until the right moment to make a move. Some corporate leaders may indeed fear the existence of such subordinates, jealously guarding their territory and accolades to ensure a strong wall of protection from the rebels below. But, I see this perspective more in the world of volunteers than in a corporate setting.

Community organizations, church committees, civic leagues—many of these groups feature long-standing leaders who have created their own little kingdoms. They have gained a sense of personal accomplishment or communal acclaim through their year-after-year commitment. Sadly, these kinds of leaders often feel jealous and suspicious, viewing followers as a threat if they are a little too zealous, a little too involved, a little too independent or accomplished. (This perspective might also result from a misunderstood or misapplied sense of ownership—see Chapter 7.)

~~Misconception: Followers Are Lemmings~~

Reality: Followers Are Achievers

Followers are not mindless rodents that have potential only for robot-like utility. Followers are valuable people, just like leaders, with our own talents, experiences, and knowledge that can supplement and complement the leader's vision and abilities. Leaders who have well-developed, engaged followers can benefit from tremendous relationships and become far more than any seminar ever promised they could be.

But our struggle with lemming identity often runs deeper. When we internalize this external view, we may develop a single drive: productivity. So what if I lack vision? What does it matter if I don't see the big picture? Maybe I *am* a bit mindless and like to be told what to do. At least I can be productive. At least I can assert my worth by putting up outstanding performance numbers and output levels.

I have felt this kind of internal evaluation, felt myself being driven to produce to make up for any sense of failure attached to holding a follower role. For me, the way forward involved a proper understanding of rest (more to come on this in Chapter 13). The remedy for viewing ourselves as machines is to realize that life is not created for the sole purpose of productivity. We are so much more.

But part of this stereotype also includes the notion that some authority figures may actually want followers to live and work as lemmings—to obey, to accept the status quo, and to reject independent thought and action. You've probably encountered or at least read about such leaders (check your history book!). These leaders get an ego boost at seeing how vital they are, how many "lemmings" utterly depend upon their leadership for productivity, value, safety, and survival.

The irony in the Lemmings game, however, is that the lemmings themselves become the tools to affect their own salvation. Given the right combination of tasks and resources, they build bridges, demolish walls, and even sacrifice themselves for the good of their compatriots. Achieving the goal and progressing to the next level require the activity of both leaders and "lemmings."

~~Misconception: Followers Are Unqualified to Be Leaders~~

Reality: Followers Are Not Second-Class Contributors

My heart was truly delighted when I attended a leadership development program at which a few of the attendees were not currently leaders and had no specific desire to become leaders. These people were not in the "emerging leader" category, and yet they were deemed worthy of an investment of resources because they would take their knowledge and use it for the benefit of the teams on which they served.

Such opportunities are scarce because of the ever-looming debate on the effective use of resources. All too often, "the prevailing idea in some circles seems to be that the only [ones] worth equipping are those the current leaders think will one day become leaders."[3] And while it's true that resources are limited, and wise leaders should be concerned about training those who may eventually replace them, the consistent giving of resources and opportunities to others becomes a problem when it disempowers followers.

When we feel disempowered, aspects of our character that we consider virtues may suddenly feel like points of failure, as when "sometimes people misunderstand meekness and think that it is weakness."[4] We may think, "Am I in a different league than the bright, shining stars who seem to be on everyone's radar for future leadership greatness?" We wonder whether we're being overlooked for having the wrong set of qualities and attributes and ask, "Am I too quiet, humble, or non-confrontational?"

One author made this rather shaking statement: "What we like to call 'making mistakes' is another name for following."[5] At first read, we may take this statement as further evidence of the myth that followers are low quality, and readily derive the equations that faultless = leader, and mistake-ridden = follower.

However, there is actually an encouragement for us here, a freeing sense of reality: Mistakes are part of life; they are part of involvement; they are inescapable for anyone who contributes—leaders and followers alike. If we are going to participate in any committee, team, group, or organization, we are going to make mistakes—whether it's misfiling an important document or stammering when speaking in front of others.

Rather than hide any weakness, rather than finding someone else to blame, we can become healthier, more effective contributors by letting go of the lie that we are innately lesser quality—and that if we weren't somehow less, we would be the ones in leadership roles.

> "Being a follower implies action. I am a follower, not a sitter, stander, or sleeper" (*Follower First*, 86).

We can take this concept a step further in realizing that it is vital for us as followers to be of extremely high quality. We may think of leaders as possessing an array of admirable attributes, but it is important for us to realize this simple fact: "The stronger the leader, the stronger and smarter the follower must be to successfully support and execute the necessary tasks."[6] If followers were of inherently poor quality, then no excellent leaders would ever have the appropriate human resources available to accomplish the vision, projects, and tasks of the organization or team. Rather, it is essential that we, as followers, both pursue and exhibit excellence in our contribution so that we can provide adequate—no, exemplary—support to those who are directing our group efforts.

As a fan of the Lemmings computer game, I can attest that after hours of playing, I—the leader-director of my tribe of creatures—became nearly as mindless as the on-screen rodents: I could give them their orders and then sit idly as they completed their tasks.

A two-way relationship in which both followers and leaders exhibit the very best qualities relevant to their roles is much more beneficial. It's not that a strong leader compensates for weak and mindless followers, but rather that capable leaders can achieve even more when their excellent followers offer the the fullness of who they are—their skills, their experience, and their perspective. Within such a dynamic, leaders and followers alike are able to exhibit the best they have to offer.

What's more, I've met many leaders who feel burdened and distracted. Some of them have shared that they often desire to set aside their leadership mantle and return to the work they enjoyed doing. Perhaps such a perspective is unique within the non-profit sector, but nonetheless, it seems that a life invested purely in pursuing leadership could surface another flavor of discontentment. Rather than providing more opportunities for meaningful work, becoming a leader may instead hinder engagement in the kinds of tasks and relationships that followers prefer and are skilled for. Followers are free of many of the stresses and challenges that can prevent leaders from doing the work they most love. Whatever thoughts I had about leadership as the standard of evaluation diminished when I realized that no title alone could guarantee job satisfaction.

~~Misconception: Being a Follower Is the Polar Opposite of Being a Leader~~

Reality: Followers Are Defined by What They Are (Not What They Are Not)

I took an online survey in December 2012 that was designed to identify whether I had the gift of leadership.[7] Among the characteristics evaluated were the following: feels the thrill of a challenge, constantly seeks a better way to do things, identifies ideas that are practical from those that are not, excited by responsibility, completes projects, can withstand criticism and act independently, receives the respect of others, has the support of family, listened to by others, and accepts reasonable mistakes. Browsing these attributes, I found myself wondering if these were really sufficient marks for identifying leaders.

I completed the survey a number of times—both honestly, for myself, and while imagining what the survey writers might consider as an ideal leader. My ideal leader responses produced this result: "This person *definitely* shows leadership traits. Immediately find ways to integrate them into your team." My honest, less "leaderly" responses produced results that said I needed further development or that my various deficiencies should be noted and addressed.

Clearly, there is a pervasive perception that leaders exhibit a certain set of characteristics and that a lack of those traits—or the presence of opposite traits—relegates one to follower (non-leader) status. But in rethinking this survey, I began to wonder what leader wouldn't want to see these same characteristics in a high-quality follower. Accomplishing tasks? Discerning practical from impractical approaches? Garnering the respect of coworkers and family? Admitting mistakes and accepting criticism?

Because many cultures elevate leaders, according them special status and privileges, it is understandable that there would be a checklist of sorts by which to identify those who are leaders—and those who are not. Author Rusty Ricketson[8] compiled such checklists from the works of leadership guru John C. Maxwell: (1) "Followers tell you what you want to hear. Leaders tell you what you need to hear"; (2) "Followers will always weigh the advantage/disadvantage issue in light of personal gain/loss, not organizational gain/loss"; (3) followers cannot navigate on their own, leaders must navigate for them; (4) followers cannot sufficiently get things done, only leaders accomplish tasks.

We often consider leaders to be those who have made something of themselves, those who have developed their natural abilities to a significant degree so that they qualify for leadership. Followers, then, are those who haven't made the effort to improve or who didn't have the raw talent and leadership attributes to begin with.

What is the remedy for this misconception? The simple acknowledgment that "followers also invent themselves."[9] That is, followers, too, make intentional choices about who they are, how they grow, and the manner in which they execute their roles. We cannot regard followers as merely non-leaders.

And there is yet another perspective from which we can derive value. The term "polar opposite" (as used in the corresponding misconception) can actually be helpful to us. Think about magnets, which have a north and south pole. The famous dictum "opposites attract" reminds us that the south pole of one magnet will adhere to the north pole of another. When they bond, a new, larger magnet is formed—one with greater potential.

> "Curiously, counterintuitively, what it takes to be a good follower looks a lot like what it takes to be a good leader" (Kellerman, *Followership*, 236).

As we consider leaders and followers, we see that all people have their own deficiencies and needs. Where one lacks, another may have great skill, ability, or experience. In this way, leaders and followers may be different from one another, not in quality, but as complements. Perhaps a leader has vision, but needs human resources to see it accomplished; followers can meet that need. Similarly, a follower may have vision, but lacks the appropriate platform from which to share it or to garner the needed resources; here, leaders can help.

Leadership and followership are obviously different, but the quality of people who serve in those roles—their natural abilities, learned skills, perspectives, and experiences—are not hard-wired into a given title. Followers may be unlike leaders in the nature of their contributions, yes. But are they complete opposites in the sense of quality, personality, or potential? Not at all.

~~Misconception: Followers Only Follow to Get Ahead~~

Reality: Excellent Followers Act with Integrity and Commitment

In an age where the existence of true altruism is being examined as a myth, the notion that we might want to be involved for the good of others, the accomplishment of the vision, and the betterment of the organization can be a hard sell. This is not to say that all followers are without leadership ambition or that all followers are altruistic. But if we desire to be good followers, to contribute and participate with excellence in our various communal associations, then we must act with integrity and authenticity.

While some, perhaps many, types of followers are attracted to the specific person of the leader,[10] the myth that followers follow only to get ahead touches on the notion that followers may be obsessed with the position of leader and achieving it for themselves.

Instead of fixating on a particular leader or leadership role, followers have the option of living with their organization's common purpose as the object of their motivation and intention, happily remaining in a follower role if that provides the best opportunity for fulfilling that purpose. As Ira Chaleff says, "Followers and leaders both orbit around the purpose; followers do not orbit around the leader."[11] Personally embracing the centrality of a common purpose is one thing—conveying it to leaders can be another, especially to leaders who may prefer lemmings and who feel threatened by your devotion to excellent followership.

It may be useful to keep yet another perspective in mind, and to communicate this to our leaders as well: Followership, while it can certainly be an influential role, is fundamentally a "willingness, ability or capacity to be influenced. ... True followership is an act of one's will ... a choice."[12] We should enter into our supporting roles with a posture of openness, offering integrity and intentionality as a participant and as a learner, submitting our ability to contribute to the guidance and direction of someone who has a similar aim, with whom we share a common purpose.

Followers are not senseless sheep duped into mediocrity. We are willing contributors who enter into a relationship that will require some sacrifice of our independence and some self-determination to achieve our purpose. To approach a threatened leader with such a humble perspective—offered with integrity and authenticity—is to open the door for incredible levels of collaboration and contribution. To ease a leader's fear of being upstaged will also lay the foundation for an essential attribute of excellent followership: trust.

4

LEADERSHIP
ACCORDING TO FOLLOWERS

Let's return to our internal perceptions as followers. Just as our inner thoughts about ourselves—our value, our personality, our goals—can affect our ability to be effective, excellent followers, so too our outwardly directed thoughts about leadership can shape our circumstances and relationships in a way that can hinder us from giving our fullest and best contribution.

Misconception: Leaders Are Superior Versions of Followers

Prevailing cultural images reinforce the view that leaders are heroes, larger-than-life figures who achieve beyond the ability of mere followers, and we may feel pressured to aspire to a leadership role, spending all of our efforts in emulating our leaders.

But this misconception goes beyond identifying positive role models and seeking to adopt their habits. Taken to the extreme, this belief could manifest as celebrity worship or membership in a leader's personality cult. More commonly this misconception twists our expectations of our leaders. If we believe they are superior versions of ourselves/followers, then we also tend to think we should be striving to do the same work that they are doing. Or, from the opposite perspective, we may believe that they should be doing the same work we are.

Misconception: Leaders Must Be Perfect

If we believe leaders are superior, we may approach the extreme notion that leaders should not only exhibit expertise in every area, but that they should perform their roles with perfection, flawlessly communicating and executing their array of decision-making tasks.

We often demand perfection from our leaders, believing that one mistake should disqualify a person from leadership. Once we conclude that a person merits a leadership role, we judge his or her ongoing suitability by the testament of an unblemished record.

From a place of defeated followership, we may come to believe that all leaders also have a history free from mistakes or errors—or we at least assume they've been able to keep any major faults to a minimum. And in that vein, we tend to think our own imperfections are holding us back, causing others to devalue us. We face an uphill battle in rescuing ourselves from such a perspective.

Misconception: Hierarchy Is Inherently Inhibiting

Sometimes we give ourselves permission to make sub-standard contributions because we believe we are victims of the system— that the reality of hierarchy prevents us from contributing all that we have anyway.

This misconception relies on the belief that the structure is inherently unjust, or that it's an antiquated approach in an era when egalitarianism and "flat" organizations are idealized. We also subscribe to this misconception when we believe hierarchy prevents us from receiving acknowledgment for all that we've done.

Misconception: Followers Don't *Really* Need Leaders

We may conclude that we should simply do away with hierarchy and structure, not only because it can be limiting, but also because we see that leaders are people too—as prone to mistakes as anyone else.

If we don't buy in to the misconception that leaders are perfect, we might end up at the opposite end of the spectrum wondering: Why do I even need leaders at work, in my community, or at my church? I can point to aspects of my life in which I function quite well without leaders. If we are all created equal and I'm capable and self-sufficient, then what do leaders have that I need?

~~Misconception: Leaders Are Superior Versions of Followers~~

Reality: Leaders and Followers Fulfill Different Roles

At its heart, the leadership-followership dynamic is about division of labor. In any project and for every organization, there are various tasks to do, decisions to be made, relationships to navigate, items to communicate. Followers handle some of these tasks while leaders take care of others.

For instance, responsibility for representing the organization is most likely appropriate for a leader—someone who has authority and is empowered to speak, negotiate, and decide on behalf of the organization. Likewise, drafting a leaflet or flyer for publication may best be handled by a follower who can capture and articulate the heart and realities of the organization to a broad audience.[1] Coming to terms with this sense of difference allows great freedom for our leaders and us as followers.

Acknowledging these role distinctions can also keep us from overstepping our bounds by trying to transform follower roles into miniaturized leadership positions.

Jimmy Collins, former president of the Chick-fil-A fast-food chain, offers this perspective: "The boss has a different job than the workers, and the boss should not be doing the same job as the workers. There may be times when employees think the boss is doing nothing when they compare it to what they are doing ... but employees should realize that if a boss is duplicating the tasks the workers are doing, then the boss is neglecting the job the boss is being paid to do. In this situation, a follower will help the boss get back to her leadership position, doing her own work."[2]

What's more, I recently read about Danish entrepreneur Tommy Ahlers.[3] He has successfully started a number of software companies. With his leadership, these companies have grown to the point of being acquired by larger corporations for many millions of dollars. All the while, Mr. Ahlers has admitted that he's really not very good at computer programming.

Some followers see this as unjust: How can an inept programmer be given leadership over an entire computer firm? Because leadership and followership are different roles, requiring different skills. Leaders do not need to be the best at doing the same work as followers; they need to understand that work, but should focus their efforts on being the best at what *they* do.

I currently find myself in the midst of such a situation. As an area leader for a non-profit, I support and oversee a number of team leaders, each of whom is serving in a role that I myself have never held. While I sometimes wish that I had that

> "Followership is perceived as a forced condition of servitude that impedes individuality and results in the loss of identity of the person following" (*Discovering Followership*, 1).

experience as part of my résumé, so as to better relate to their needs, my lack of personal familiarity with serving in a team leader role hasn't precluded me from leading leaders. After all, my oversight role requires different skills and perspectives than the on-the-ground leadership roles do; my day-to-day tasks include things like large-scale communication, navigating the big picture, and administration—things that most team leaders don't have to touch. I want to understand team leaders so that I can effectively support them, but interestingly (and thankfully), my lack of specific prior experience didn't dissuade my boss or my current subordinates from welcoming me into this role. They already know the truth that we're after: Leadership and followership roles are different.

As one example, I may have actually been a rather lousy team leader, whereas I feel reasonably effective within my overseeing/support role. If we believe that our leaders are simply superior, higher-profile versions of ourselves, we may overlook the right candidate for the right job. We should instead focus on placing people in their best-fitting roles—by looking at the various skills, abilities, experience, and perspective they can bring.

~~Misconception: Leaders Must Be Perfect~~

Reality: Leaders Are People Too

In case you haven't yet come around, I'll repeat this truth once more: Leaders are people too. It's unreasonable for us to expect them or anyone, regardless of role, to be without fault. We all make mistakes. We misjudge, misspeak, and misunderstand. We allow stress from other areas of our lives to creep into our roles, and we react emotionally when we should act with compassion and empathy.

Furthermore, we can and should expect our leaders to blunder, to err, and to be blatantly wrong, and we must offer understanding and support in these moments. Relationships with our leaders remind us of the realities of our shared humanity and correct our unreasonable expectations.

~~Misconception: Hierarchy Is Inherently Inhibiting~~

Reality: Well-Conceived Hierarchy Is Healthy and Empowering

Structure can be freeing. While some people may believe that any sense of formality or rigidity is inherently limiting, having a framework actually presents great opportunities for freedom.

For example, I find a household budget to be one of the most freeing aspects of my daily life. Where some of my friends may see financial handcuffs—categories and line items that limit spending and spontaneity—for me, the spreadsheet has opened up a new perspective on how my wife and I use our monetary resources.

I find myself more generous with charitable giving, less anxious about spending money on date night, and more excited about Christmas shopping when I realize that this structure has allotted resources for each of these outlets. Because of budgeting, vacation, the occasional surprise bouquet of flowers for my wife, and even the unexpected expense of helping someone in need can be met with joy and anticipation rather than anxiety and cost-benefit analysis.

Likewise, a well-shaped organization can provide freedom both to leaders and to followers. When people have clarity about their roles, they gain implicit permission and encouragement to fully engage in their own tasks while entrusting other work to other people. A clear sense of my role, and of others' roles (including my leader's), can create an environment that is not *oppressive*, but rather *expressive* of the very best I have to offer my group, team, or community.

History is replete with examples of stifling, oppressive regimes, and perhaps you are working within a circumstance that feels similarly. But that doesn't invalidate the utility of hierarchy, structure, and division of labor. It takes significant effort to achieve a healthy structure, but doing so creates empowering opportunities.

I attended a leadership development event a few years ago, and I was very impressed to hear a group of leaders indicate the need for a team member/follower role description. They had a document outlining all of the formal leadership roles, those leaders' various responsibilities, and the organization's expectations for them. But for team members—by far the largest portion of the organization—they had no similar document, and they had realized the gravity of this gap.

This parallel document was drafted not only to communicate specific expectations—areas of involvement and responsibility the leaders depended on—but to validate the team member role. What an encouraging example of how we might move toward healthy, freeing hierarchy! We should applaud and emulate an organization that creates an environment based on acknowledging and valuing various roles, while intentionally addressing members at every level to clarify requirements, expectations, and opportunities.

An even more significant remedy to the issues of hierarchy is to deepen our engagement with it. More precisely, the way forward is not to entrench ourselves within the structure for structure's sake, but to invest in the *people* who constitute that structure.

Researcher Larry Hirschhorn advocates for this type of relational engagement within our groups: "I suggest that the post-modern enterprise embraces hierarchy but enlivens it with feelings and passion. It strengthens hierarchy by personalizing it. Only the enlivened hierarchy—one in which superiors and subordinates can work across recognized authority boundaries while retaining their distinctive roles—can suppress [unhelpful, limiting, hindering] bureaucracy."[4]

Passion and commitment—the fundamentals of relationship—lead to a structure that is "enlivened," one that is life-giving and facilitates the very best involvement from all. Rather than pretending structure doesn't exist, or presuming that it is inherently ineffective, we can use structure as an opportunity for better relationships, both with our fellow followers and with our leaders.

By understanding each other's contributions—on a personal level and in the grand scheme of the organization—we can find freedom to fully engage in the work that we do, while allowing others to do the same. (We will have much more to say about this kind of relationship with our leaders and with other followers in later chapters.)

~~Misconception: Followers Don't Really Need Leaders~~

Reality: Followers and Leaders Need Each Other

Do we really need leaders? The root of the misconception that we do not need leaders lies in the notion that we are all independent and self-sustaining individuals who tend to our own needs and fulfill our own purposes. In reality, of course, we are not self-sufficient. Neither leaders nor followers can rightfully adopt this perspective.

It's not uncommon to talk about being part of something that is bigger than ourselves. The heart of this sense of belonging is that there are dreams, opportunities, and goals that outstrip us as individuals. We cannot accomplish them alone, nor are we alone in valuing them; other people also have a vision to support or achieve in the same way that we do.

As mature adults, we have a great array of capabilities within ourselves. We have learned skills for living life and performing our work. We have learned how to communicate and make decisions for ourselves. We take responsibility for our actions.

While we *can* do these things, we may find an incredible opportunity in not *having* to do these things on our own. For instance, my emails are better when someone else proofreads them.

I make better decisions when someone else shares his or her perspective with me. My soul is more at ease when I don't bear responsibility alone.

Admitting that we need leaders—that leadership is useful to us as followers—opens us up to taking advantage of the resources that are available in community. If we see leaders as simply the peddlers of vision, then we may easily enough dismiss their value: "I don't need someone to tell me what's important to me."

Instead, if we regard leaders (and organizations) as an avenue for pursuing what we value, believe in, and dream of, then we can enter into that leader-follower relational dynamic with a sense of mutual benefit and contribution. As we find that others share our motivation, we realize our efforts can be maximized through the coordination, perspective, and representation that leaders can provide.

I know of teams who engage in highly nuanced work in far-flung locations. Within our organization, there are only a few people working in the same way. Through the networks created by leaders—both within and beyond our own organization—such teams have been brought into contact with others who have similar drive and experience. Because the leaders got involved, the team's purpose can now be fueled through these new connections.

> "Followers and leaders have different perspectives because of their relative position in the organizational structure" (*Power of Followership*, 185).

When we admit that we need leaders, we will eventually realize that leaders also need us. Leaders have their own vision and passions and motivations, but they cannot accomplish the work all on their own. At the very least, followers can do the nuts and bolts work needed to fulfill a leader's grand aim. More so, followers are people with talents and experience that come into play in the accomplishment of complicated and worthwhile endeavors. As John Donne taught us, "No man is an island"—neither leaders nor followers—"every man is piece of the continent, a part of the main"—together creating the greatness of an effective organization.

Summarizing Chart

As mentioned at the outset of this book, our aim is to determine how we can engage in our followership role with excellence. In the exploration of the misconceptions in the previous chapters, we have seen a number of perspectives—both internal and external—that can prevent us from contributing our very best. These misconceptions and the ideas they've surfaced will form the basis for much of our exploration in the chapters to come. The following chart summarizes these misconceptions for easy reference.

Misconception	Reality	Remedy
Leadership is the goal of followership.	Followership is intrinsically valuable.	Realizing that leaders are people too, and finding a sense of "enoughness"—just the right situation for us to use our talents and make our unique contributions
I'm a follower because I'm a coward.	Being an excellent follower takes courage.	Owning the truth that part of our role is to confront, communicate, and decide ... even in our interactions with leaders

Misconception	Reality	Remedy
Followers have no authority or influence.	Followers can exert real influence.	Embracing freedom by separating influence from authority and recognition
Followership lacks honor and dignity.	Followers are noble and worthy of respect.	Valuing our associations with others and separating out inappropriate cultural expectations
Followers are lemmings.	Followers are achievers.	Acknowledging the significance of what you have to contribute and finding freedom from engaging in mere productivity
Followers are unqualified to be leaders.	Followers are not second-class contributors.	Admitting that we all have imperfections and yet we are all essential, with much to contribute that is necessary
Being a follower is the polar opposite of being a leader.	Followers are defined by what they are (not what they are not).	Intentionally working to develop ourselves, choosing our involvements, and identifying our purpose and aims
Followers only follow to get ahead.	Excellent followers act with integrity and commitment.	Expressing authenticity in your desire to serve, participate, and contribute

Misconception	Reality	Remedy
Leaders are superior versions of followers.	Leaders and followers fulfill different roles.	Pursuing clarity in role distinctions and job descriptions
Leaders must be perfect.	Leaders are people too.	Establishing the same expectations for your leaders as for yourself, including permission to make mistakes
Hierarchy is inherently inhibiting.	Well-conceived hierarchy is healthy and empowering.	Discovering freedom through role differentiation
Followers don't really need leaders.	Followers and leaders need each other.	Correcting the untruth of self-sufficiency in your thoughts about yourself and your leaders

Part 2

CAN AND SHOULD: THE OPPORTUNITIES OF EXCELLENT FOLLOWERSHIP

If you're feeling discouraged—like the journey of following well is almost impossible—stick with me. The variety of internal and external misconceptions we just explored does indeed make it difficult for us to get a clear picture of what excellent followership looks like. And even if we have some idea, we may feel alone in our pursuit; our clubhouse, church building, or community center may seem inherently opposed to overcoming these misconceptions.

But we're just getting started. Now that we've surfaced some of these mistaken ideas about followership, we'll start to build a positive picture of what it means to follow well. It all begins with a life that overcomes the misconceptions and moves ahead with intentionality into the opportunities that we have as followers to contribute.

Such opportunities can fit broadly into two categories: obligations and contributions. Obligations are aspects of following that are necessary for us to invest in if we are to truly follow well. As you'll see, these are not so much items on a task list as they are a posture, or a perspective, from within which we fulfill our follower role. Although we may resist the term "obligations," preferring not to have a sense of requirement placed upon us, the follower role is significant *because* there are essential ways in which we *must* be involved for our group to be healthy and effective. If this weren't the case, then followers would be completely optional, unnecessary even. But that simply isn't so. We have real work to do.

We also have contributions—other ways that we can add value through our involvement (which we'll explore in Chapter 6). Engaging in these opportunities may not be required, or even expected, but going above and beyond the minimum will open the door for us to follow with excellence.

Taken together, these chapters on obligations and contributions will help to give us a more concrete framework as we explore excellent followership.

5

OBLIGATIONS OF FOLLOWERSHIP

Followers Must Participate

The most fundamental aspect of following is simply this: to participate. By its very nature, the follower role is one that expresses our attachment to a group endeavor. There are other people involved: one or more leaders and likely other followers as well. We engage in this association in order to achieve something—create profit, plan an event, win a trophy, provide humanitarian relief. For our follower role to have any meaning at all, we must begin by participating.

We must ask ourselves: "What does it mean to offer my services?"[1] Answering that question includes understanding what it means to be involved. Why are you a part of the team or group or congregation, and what are you there to do? Ask yourself: "How can I contribute to the accomplishments of the group and add something positive?"

These questions are at the root of followership, but they are not easy to answer and not necessarily easy to fulfill. Deciding to be involved means having to use our energy and resources; it means we'll have to cooperate, commit, compromise, converse, and perhaps change our actions and perspective.

My own journey of participation has been significant. I have always perceived myself as a bit of a loner by nature. I am fairly self-directed and independent, content to work by myself on whatever task is assigned to me. Because of this, I often struggled with social situations; I never felt like I had much to offer, and so any sort of group event—meeting, retreat, conference— was a challenge for me. Such things used up a large portion of my time and energy in exchange for marginally useful returns. I often felt like my time would be much better spent if I could just carry on with my individual plans.

It was at that point I had to catch myself and revisit the idea of my role. I was part of a team (specifically, as a team member/follower at that time), and for my role to be meaningful, I needed to be involved with what the team was doing—whether they were meeting, talking, or playing. If the team cared, I needed to care.

The challenge of participation occurs when we question the worth of the group or organization's efforts. Aside from times when there might be a moral, legal, or ethical question,[2] our followership should begin with joining in on whatever the group is doing. Involvement should be our default course of action, whether participating in team-building activities, attending long meetings, listening patiently, reading and responding to emails, being present (i.e., not doing other work) during conference calls, or participating in other activities that we may not naturally be inclined to value. Excellence in following begins with showing up, not just as a lukewarm body, but as a person with something to contribute— whether that's a pair of hands, an insight, or a question.

> "The model [of courageous followership] speaks to our courage, power, integrity, responsibility, and sense of service"
> (*The Courageous Follower*, 1).

One tool that facilitates my own participation is an agenda; knowing what's happening helps me to set expectations and to prepare myself to have something to offer. I have often had leaders who invited input on the agenda-creation process. For me, this was a clear opportunity to shape my team, to express the things I valued, and to encourage conversations about items I thought were significant. I felt frustrated when the leader solicited and welcomed such input and yet no one responded. As a result, no agenda was shared ahead of time, and I was unable to effectively prepare and contribute. Our failure to participate led to difficult meetings and made the whole experience of involvement more challenging.

In addition, the team discussions weren't as effective as they could have been since the team members hadn't voiced the topics that they considered essential. Even the wisest of leaders can't see every detail, and they certainly can't know every concern. So being remiss in participation lessened the effectiveness of these team-meeting times, which then served to enforce feelings that such meetings were a waste of time.

The lesson for me was *participate! Contribute something!* I may not have incredible insight or a perfect grasp of the big picture, but I can offer some input, some perspective, some ideas that add value. In fact, we can push this notion even further; as one executive expressed, "Tight-mouthed workers who do not express their point of view are in a sense 'stealing' the intellectual inventory of the organization by not openly sharing."[3]

To fail to voice our thoughts, or to hold back our involvement, is not simply to let opportunities for input pass us by, but can actually hinder or hurt our organization. An organization is people—the human resources are its defining factor—and for us not to engage is to steal those resources. Participation is an obligation.

Political systems offer us a similar challenge. Many cultures espouse the virtues of democracy, yet overlook a fundamental aspect of it. "Democratic followers ... are presumed to be prepared to participate."[4] For a democracy to work, its people must actually be involved in the process. In the U.S., many people bemoan the ineffectiveness and ineptitude of the political system. But the system is so lackluster, in part, because many citizens have abdicated their involvement, which results in a democratic system that has lost most of its human resources and relies instead on a scant few hundreds of politicians to make decisions on behalf of hundreds of millions of people.

As Harvard leadership and government professor Barbara Kellerman observes, "Young people today do not think of followership, of citizenship, as entailing obligations of any kind, including voting."[5] I would suggest that this is not only true of the young, and not only true in the realm of citizenship and government. People in general—members of all sorts of groups—do not consider their attachment to include any kind of obligation.

If we look intently, we can identify all manner of dysfunction in our businesses and communities; while it has often been our practice to label the reason for this ineffectiveness as a crisis of leadership, it is probably more accurate to say that we are routinely facing crises of followership.[6] I am convinced that the first step in remedying these crises is for followers to participate, to fully engage, to contribute, to do what the group is doing, to employ resources, words, and perspective in the fulfillment of the group's aims and with the goal of enhancing the effectiveness of all involved.

Followers Must Steward Their Resources and Opportunities

The concept of stewardship has dominated much of my thinking on followership. This idea was well developed by the Middle Ages, when kings and other aristocrats owned vast estates, consisting of a substantial workforce and an array of business ventures—farms, textile mills, and all manner of trade and commerce.

A single estate had too many resources for one man to manage, especially if he was expected to spend most of his time mingling with society and enjoying his wealth. So these estate owners appointed stewards—someone who didn't share any of the ownership, but was given the responsibility for making good use of the resources and managing the affairs so as to be profitable.

Within the realm of humanity, we are all stewards. Regardless of whether we have substantial economic resources, we all have time, talents, energy, gifts, abilities, skills, knowledge, wisdom, insight, experience, passion, perspective, values, and vision that we can put to use. We also have the choice not to use these things, and to allow them—and ourselves—to remain idle and ineffective, unprofitable either for our own aims or in fulfillment of others' goals.

This idea of stewardship is a natural outflow of the basic notion of participation. With intentionality and consideration, we look at what we have available to us and determine which of these resources to employ in the various projects, organizations, and efforts in which we are involved. It is up to us to make excellent use of these assets, but doing so does not happen automatically.

A good beginning is to appreciate the value of our follower role. As I noted in Chapter 2, it is common for many of us as followers to undervalue our own contribution and influence. If we don't believe that we have much opportunity to make a difference or have worthwhile involvement, then we will naturally gravitate toward poor stewardship.

On the other hand, if we sense that our followership role affords us opportunities to contribute to our group's goals, then we will have reason to use our personal resources in seeing those purposes realized—thus moving into the realm of good, effective stewardship. Rather than letting our abilities wither away and collect dust, we can put them to work to produce, achieve, impact, and support.

"Support" is another notion that has been influential in my own followership. Several times I have served in assistant-type roles. In such a follower position, it was clear to me that one of my main functions was to support the work of the leader, but also the work of the larger team that I was a part of.

This fits well with the etymologies of the words "follower" and "leader," as traced by Robert Kelley. He observes that "follower" means "to assist, help, ... or minister to. This parallels the ... root of 'leader,' which meant to undergo, suffer, or endure."[7] In even more straightforward terms: "The reason why you are there as a follower is to help your leader to accomplish the task at hand."[8] This perspective contrasts a bit with Ira Chaleff's statement on courageous following: "In my model, followers don't serve leaders—that's an intentionally provocative statement. Both followers and leaders serve the mission, and they are both accountable for doing so according to a shared set of values."[9] While the heart of Chaleff's statement is likely true, my experience is that the reality of serving the organization's goal may indeed mean serving and supporting the leader in ways that are less grand and not so directly related to achieving the overarching purpose.

A followership role is an opportunity to provide support for both our leaders and our fellow followers. We are part of a network of support, a reservoir of resources, and by applying ourselves to the right tasks and relationships in the right ways, we can contribute to completing the work at hand and to creating a manageable environment where the work would otherwise be overwhelming.

What does support look like from a practical perspective? What might our good stewardship lead us to do? Communication is one avenue of support. Regardless of our levels of expertise, we can all communicate. Regardless of whether we have an impressive résumé or unique skill set, we can always share our thoughts. As Michael Useem notes, "If we want to serve our superiors, whose mission we support, our responsibility is to furnish them with strategic insight, timely advice, and realistic opinions when their future is on the line."[10]

Note that there is a *responsibility* here, an obligation. Our followership roles become something substantive when we communicate with our leaders. We can steward our thoughts, words, and perspective by contributing when needed.

Sometimes the moment of need isn't realized by our leaders. Although we may at times be consulted or invited into a dialogue (as I was given the opportunity for input into my team's agenda-creation process), at other times we may have to express excellent stewardship by appropriately volunteering information and perspective when it isn't requested.

> "Leaders are responsible for what happens—and followers are as well" (Kellerman, *Followership*, 73).

Michael Useem, who provides a number of historical examples of the vital role played by followers and their willingness to influence the leaders above them, reminds us, "It is your solemn duty—and in this case a sacred one—to give your best counsel, render your best judgment, and persist in the expression of both, whether such upward leadership is specifically sought or not."[11] In later chapters, we will further explore the crucial value of having a healthy relationship with your leader when determining how to offer such unsolicited support.

One way to initiate supportive communication with your leader is to ask a very simple question: "How are you doing?"[12] Checking on your superior to determine his or her current needs and what struggles and difficulties she or he might be encountering creates an opportunity for our stewardship to have great effect.

If we offer this question sincerely—along with asking "how can I help?"—it can be powerful indeed, both for the leader in need and for the follower who wants to act with good stewardship in mind. With this offer of support, our role as followers and our leaders' roles may surprisingly become both doable and life-giving, rather than hopeless and overwhelming.

Other ways to show good stewardship and supportive communication include speaking truthfully to one's superiors. Ensuring that a leader has correct information, that he or she is aware of relevant factors, and that together there is a realistic picture of what is happening, are all fundamental ways that a follower can be involved in a valuable support role. Exercising poor stewardship is to let data go uncorrected, to allow errant thinking to persist, and to sugarcoat or distort what's actually happening.

To function as a good steward may at times require saying difficult things, reminding others of our organizations' values, or even pointing out mistakes that have been made.[13] This too is best done in the context of a healthy relationship to ensure that we, even with good intentions, don't offend others or put them on the defensive when we talk about sensitive issues.

Beyond the realm of communication, our basic inclination as followers who steward our resources well involves the simple idea of faithfully fulfilling our role and responsibilities. The heart of excellence in followership lies in doing the work that has been entrusted to us and applying whichever of our resources may be required. If we are not dependable, then we seriously undercut the possibility that our followership platform will enable us to make positive contributions to our organization's efforts. All the good intentions and all the amazing potential within us ultimately count for very little if we are negligent in doing what we have committed to do.

For some people, the challenge of stewardship comes from a present discontent and fixation on the future. If we are primarily focused on a promotion or on eventually occupying the leader's chair, then we may be tempted to disengage from current opportunities. We may convince ourselves that we are saving our time, energy, and other resources for when we have "real work" to do (when we attain that coveted position), or we may downplay the value of our current tasks, dismissing the need for our participation.

However, if followers are constantly holding back, waiting for other opportunities, discontent with the work assigned to them, and unappreciative of the significance of seemingly mundane tasks, then the group's efforts will suffer. We must faithfully steward our roles—whether as followers or as leaders—for our organization to achieve the height of its effectiveness. If we choose not to be good stewards within our current roles, we will be removing our unique contribution from play, and the ramifications of that choice are real—both for us and for the community with which we are involved.

Followers Must Honor Their Leaders

As we pursue being good stewards, we may have a tendency to isolate ourselves, to put up protective barriers—emotionally and relationally—in an effort to carve out a distraction-free zone where no one else can thwart our efforts at making our best contributions. We may think that we can do our best work if we could just be left alone, unencumbered by the intrusions of others—especially their opinions and mistakes.

But this kind of thinking can often lead to us establishing our own little kingdoms—our personal realms where we exist as the sole authority figure. As we become entrenched in this manner of operating, we'll find that we don't just err in making too much of ourselves while *ignoring* everyone else; we think too much of ourselves and think *negatively* about everyone else, especially our leaders.

Our perspective about others' value diminishes as we focus solely on our own accomplishments. It's easy to lose the sense that we are part of a group, and we may view our leader with suspicion or disdain as he or she attempts to influence our activity and perhaps receives praise for our contributions.

To keep this tendency in check, we have an additional obligation: Followers must honor their leaders. In our efforts to make the very most of our personal resources, we cannot lose sight of this obligation, or we risk coloring all of our well-intentioned efforts with the muck of hyper-individualism, territorialism, and arrogance.

Fundamental notions of basic human dignity should lead us to treat one another with at least a minimal amount of respect. Just as we derive encouragement from being listened to by others, from seeing our opinions valued, from feeling that our interaction and involvement is significant, we should extend that same kindness to others, especially to our leaders who— perhaps surprisingly—are also in need of encouragement and affirmation, and who rarely receive authentic expressions of appreciation.

Honor builds trust, and trust is the core of the leader-follower dynamic. "Trust is a subtle state between two people formed from an assessment of each other's internal motives and external actions."[14] For a healthy, cooperative working relationship, we must establish trust based on positive feelings toward one another and by acting in accordance with those feelings. As followers, we can make a huge contribution to the creation of trust if we feel and express honor toward our leaders.

> "An open flow of information and an open display of respect are essential"
> (*Leading Up*, 37).

We can start by appreciating the burdens and responsibilities carried by our leaders. I've had some superiors—from department chairs to team leaders—whose basic roles did not seem very different from my own. Like me, they taught courses, answered emails, made conference calls, and traveled internationally.

Yet despite this significant overlap, I noticed these leaders were often working much longer hours than I was. I simply believed they lived with less margin in their lives. It wasn't until I asked about other things they had to deal with that I was able to understand the differences between my role and theirs. Hearing about all of the other projects, discussions, and meetings they were obligated to as part of their position explained why their time and energy seemed stretched so much more than my own.

Every leader-follower situation is different, and organizations have great variation in how much similarity there is between leader and follower roles. However much your role seems to resemble your leader's, ask about the differences. You may be surprised to find out about the vast array of other tasks and responsibilities your leader carries that you had previously been unaware of. Not only will this provide you with new ways to contribute (see next chapter), but it will help you work toward honoring your leader better.

While we're on this subject, I encourage you to commit to honoring the breakroom and your relationships with other followers as well. It's easy for break times to devolve into complaining sessions about the boss. Sadly, "complaining has become acceptable in the culture. It has become the substitute for courageous, honest, and productive dialogue."[15]

In this kind of setting, it's easy to pick out the faults and mistakes of our superiors, and we may find a perverse camaraderie in collectively dishonoring our leaders. At those times, the honoring relationship that we have established with our leader should overflow into how we enter into these discussions. We can fulfill our obligation to honor our leaders when we correct the predominant voices of criticism and challenge others to consider the needs, contribution, and humanity of our leaders.

Just this morning I heard about a leader who was traveling for several weeks; he appointed an interim supervisor to provide direction during his absence. Shortly after his departure, the workers gathered and compiled a list of grievances about the leader's performance. The letter recounted wounds, misunderstandings, and mistakes. When the leader returned, he was confronted with these collected thoughts of the team, and he eventually resigned.

While some might look at this situation and accuse the team members of mutiny, I found myself asking a single question: Was there an advocate for the leader? Regardless of the mistakes made by this leader—or his responsibility to apologize, make changes, or reform—was any team member attempting to halt inflammatory groupthink? Did anyone remind the team of the leader's humanity, needs, and value? This story should challenge each of us to ask ourselves: If I were in a similar situation, would I have shown honor, care, and appreciation for my leader?

The obligation to honor should not just affect our words—to our leader *and* to our colleagues—it should affect our actions. We should find ourselves laboring diligently under and on behalf of our leader. We should work supportively, not antagonistically. The boss is not our enemy. We belong to the same organization. We are working toward the same goals. We are united by a common purpose.

We should not attempt to trample our superiors through aggressive or dismissive language, nor through negligent or belligerent attitudes. "The follower must never put himself in competition with the leader. Remember your role as the follower; your role is to work for the boss, not against the boss or in competition with the boss."[16] Acknowledging our leaders as friends, not foes, and then acting accordingly is a significant way we can display honor toward them, as we follow with excellence.

Followers Must Submit to Their Leaders

One natural outflow of honoring our leaders is allowing ourselves to be influenced. Those whom we honor, respect, value, and trust *should* have an opportunity to affect us—shaping our personal growth and the way we go about our tasks, helping us to maximize our stewardship. Being influenced in this way is one of the greatest benefits we gain from establishing a healthy follower-leader relationship.

But this open flow of influence means that we will eventually encounter expectations or decisions that we don't like. Whether we disagree or simply don't understand or don't appreciate the ramifications (like having to do work that we really dislike), we face a difficult choice: Do we go along with our leader's decision, or do we rebel? Do we do what's asked, or do we refuse? Do we accept or oppose?

As I mentioned before, there are times when we *do* need to withdraw our support (such as when moral, ethical, or legal conflicts arise), but in the majority of cases, we have a different obligation: Followers must submit to their leaders. This doesn't mean blindly following in every situation, but it does mean that our default response—barring any special concerns—should be to follow, to obey, to honor, and to participate.

We may voice concerns, offer perspective, or ask for clarification, but if the decision stands, then we need to abide by it. If it's not significant enough for us to resign, quit, or file a formal complaint with others in authority, then our continued followership should lead us to submit.

Obedience in the face of disagreement is a challenge. As children we all experienced the requirement to do things we didn't want to do. As we matured into adults and further developed our set of experiences, expectations, preferences, and habits, being forced into an unappealing course of action became only more difficult. As adults we may be better at responding with greater diplomacy and decorum (hopefully there aren't too many of us throwing tantrums!), but it still grates on us to have someone else override our will. We need self-discipline to overcome this feeling, to do what we don't want to do, to be involved in things that don't seem like our best contribution. Self-discipline will help us overcome a sense of injustice or a feeling of being ignored, helping us let go of a preference or other internal struggles we face.

Decision-making is a major component of any group dynamic. Every club, committee, or team makes decisions. Sometimes a team achieves a decision by consensus—finding a way forward based on everyone coming to agreement. However, not every decision is *or should be* made like this. And even when we do have a say, participating and offering input will not ensure that we get our way. It can be most difficult to submit in such situations.

Although it's important for us to be involved in the decision-making process, it is just as important to be involved in *decision-taking*. The first aspect of decision-taking is an internal acceptance of what has been decided. To do this, we must exert self-discipline and deal with anything that makes us feel like we've been ignored or treated unfairly.

One of our tools in this struggle is our commitment to the previous obligation: honoring our leaders. Maintaining a view of respect and trust will help us internalize the new reality—even if it has been foisted upon us—because we bring the idea of relationship into our internal reservoir of resources. If we can keep in mind the person who made this decision, policy, or requirement—our leader—we will be less likely to retaliate as if we were simply opposing an intangible, cosmic force.

If I have a healthy relationship with my leader, if I trust him or her, if I am committed to coming alongside them in the fulfillment of our mutual goals, then I can move forward without feeling that I am resigning myself to an unjust fate. In truth, I am submitting myself to someone else and allowing this person to influence my actions, which is at the heart of being a group member.

Many of the misconceptions from Part 1 will rear their ugly heads at this moment, seeking to drive a wedge between us and the effective accomplishment of our aims. We will face the temptation to devalue and dismiss our leaders, but if we are committed to honoring them as individuals and to respecting and appreciating their roles and responsibilities, then we can emerge from this struggle victorious—and ready for the second aspect of decision-taking: to put the decision into action.

Mere "compliance is activity without the whole heart."[17] Only when we have won the internal battle can we effectively implement the decision and even advocate for others to get involved. Rather than defeating an effort through our naysaying or lack of enthusiasm, we can wholeheartedly join the effort to see this hard-fought decision succeed.

> "Acts of obedience show what is in your heart; it's a choice, it's an attitude, and it may even be voluntary" (Armstrong, *Followership*, 28).

How excruciating it is when the strain of a decision-making process continues on as leadership attempts to implement that decision. When we as followers give in to our initial opposition and refuse to take the decision forward, we have failed in our followership.

As followers, "we have the responsibility to implement the policies. It takes courage to follow leaders when we are not convinced they are right, courage to truly allow leaders to lead. It is our responsibility to give the policy a chance, to make it work through energetic and intelligent adaptation rather than allow it to fail through literal interpretation or lukewarm execution. We have the right to challenge policies in the policy-making process; we do not have the right to sabotage them in the implementation phase."[18] This is exemplary decision-taking.

Beginning from an internal state of submission and acceptance, and fueled by a commitment to participate, steward, and honor, we will journey along the right track to effectively engage in this second layer of decision-taking as we work together to achieve our common goal.

Followers Must 'Be'

The core of following well is mostly about exhibiting a right attitude and perspective. I've said nothing about filing reports accurately, arriving early to all meetings, clearing out your inbox each day, or achieving performance targets. These things may be important, and they may be results or implications of following well, but our journey into excellence as followers first requires that we *be* followers.

So why did I start with what we're required to do as followers rather than first talking about who we *are*? Because in knowing what's required of a good follower, we begin to learn what a good follower is—and how to become one. What we do, the way we do it, and especially why we do it all stem from who we are. The character of our activity flows from the character of our identity.

Just as we must serve and work from an internal state that facilitates our participation, stewardship, honor, and submission in the group process, so too we must *be* in the right place—emotionally, spiritually, mentally, volitionally (will/ choices), and physically.[19] We must come with a proper perspective, fueled by a healthy attitude and energized by relationships that contribute to a constructive work environment.

Have a Right Attitude

"Leadership is a function. Followership is an identity."[20] How do these words strike you? Do you bristle at the idea, feeling a desire to blurt out, "I'm not defined by my followership!" When I first read these words, I filled the book margin with scribbled notes in an effort to clarify my perspective.

After getting my initial resentment out of my system, I took a moment to consider why I reacted the way that I did. Why am I so opposed to having an identity as a follower? The root of my outrage went back to several of the misconceptions that we explored in Part 1. Since I devalued the follower role, and evaluated myself in light of a skewed vision of leadership and followership, I naturally wanted to divorce myself from an identity that seemed to condemn me. After all, whereas a role can change, identity speaks to the core of who I am.

I still don't agree wholeheartedly with the above quotation, but I do believe there's a lesson for us here. Yes, leadership is a function, but it can also be a gifting, a stewardship, a necessary role. And followership is one source of identity, but it can also be a calling, a stewardship, a necessary role. What it really comes down to then, is our attitudes.

How do I feel about being a follower? To what degree do I own this role and identity for myself? Am I inherently resistant to it, hoping to shrug it off at the first chance I get to move on to something "bigger and better"? Or am I content, looking forward to contributing to the group's aims, committed to associating myself with others who have similar goals, and willing to persist in self-discipline, honoring others, and submission in order to see the creation of a healthy, cooperative environment for achieving our mutual purpose?

If we view our follower roles only as a burden to be endured, a punishment to serve, a purgatory through which to persevere, then we will fail to *be*: We will not be in the best place to offer our energy, engagement, wisdom, or perspective. Instead, we should embrace an attitude that leads to acceptance, ownership, and enthusiasm for our followership role. At the heart of our obligations as followers, there is a need for us to engage in our role, not with resignation and annoyance, but with interest and commitment.

Pursue Personal Development

But we have a larger pursuit as well. For us to *be* followers, we need to intentionally work on our own growth. Where do we have rough edges? When do we respond with tension? We need to push against these areas to uncover the roots that lead to our poor attitudes. On the positive side, those roots can also lead us to explore new skills and abilities, while finding new outlets for our creativity.

Personal and professional development is a must for all of us—followers as well as leaders. The majority of leadership training programs and other such resources are aimed at a small segment of the organization's makeup—leaders, emerging or established—but that doesn't permit us, as followers, to ignore our identical needs for improvement, experience, encountering fresh ideas, and acquiring new skills.

> "Followership is lifelong learning" (*I Am a Follower*, 103).

Followers offer a variety of perspectives about expectations for this kind of development. On the one hand, we read, "Leaders have failed the followers by not fulfilling their responsibility of training and providing tools for the followers' success. ... When you ask followers about some of the frustrations they have with leadership, they will tell you that the lack of training rates amongst the highest."[21] On the other hand, we find this perspective: "The responsibility to maintain leading-edge skills is yours, not the organization's. If you depend on the organization or the leader for maintaining those skills, you will be sadly disappointed."[22] So just what should we expect?

I titled this section "Pursue Personal Development" rather than "Pursue Professional Development" for a specific reason: I am thoroughly convinced that the burden of pursuing growth lies with us. Professional development is a subset of the larger journey of our transformation as an individual. We may reasonably hope for our company or organization to invest in our ongoing professional improvement by sending us to conferences, making us aware of training events, supplying us with reference materials and suggestions of best practices, and offering workplace mentoring. After all, doing so is a good investment: Improved followers should be able to contribute more effectively to the group's aims with such training.

But even if we aren't offered professional training, we still have responsibility for our own personal development. We cannot expect to "be" in the best place emotionally, spiritually, mentally, volitionally, and physically if we do not actively develop ourselves along these lines.

Although our leaders may bear much responsibility for us, we are the ones who are ultimately stewards of our life, our role, our growth. "Being"—or perhaps "becoming"—is a core obligation of all people, and certainly, all followers. We cannot make our best contributions if we delegate our development to others.

6

CONTRIBUTIONS OF FOLLOWERSHIP

Giving Credence to an Endeavor

The world is full of ideas—dreams, visions, plans, and hopes. Unending schemes and approaches for achieving various outcomes exist, and I can only guess at the number of strategy documents and five-year plans that are tucked away in desk drawers and hard drives around the world. We never hear about most of these ideas; they aren't acknowledged by the world at large. But there is one thing that can be said for all of the ideas we *do* know about, those we have seen come to reality: They involve followers.

Apart from considering any practical or tangible contributions that we may make, our involvement as followers gives credence to an endeavor. Credence is belief that something is true or real, that something actually exists. Undertakings don't exist without people who are invested in carrying them out. Once someone gets involved, the idea has evolved to actually become something—a project, an implemented plan, an organization, a team. The presence of people makes all the difference. As we followers employ hands, minds, and voices in the actuation of an idea, we make it something to acknowledge, something to respond to, something that has substance.

Followers' involvement gives weight to a cause. One person's idea can be quickly dismissed or overlooked; it's not so easy to ignore a cadre of volunteers. Once there are people behind an effort, it can move; it can affect others; it can produce and achieve. It's easy for the words of a solitary advocate to get lost in the buzz of life; it's harder to turn a deaf ear to dozens of united voices.

Practically speaking, it takes hands, minds, and energy to accomplish tasks. Human capacity is required to make things happen. But voices, values, and relationship—al-though less often sought as bottom-line resources—provide the essential contribution of bringing a purpose to life. A piece of paper defining a plan may sit idly on a desk, then get crumpled and tossed into the garbage. Followers who are participating and stewarding their involvement cannot be so easily cast aside. The focal point of their involvement and cumulative energy attracts the engagement of others.

> "But the truth is that the greatest way to create a movement is to be a follower and to show others how to follow" (*I Am a Follower*, 14).

The intentional involvement of followers generates action: line-items added to the budget, time slots assigned in agendas, resources redirected, processes redefined. An idea on a notepad is nothing without people—followers—to accomplish it.

While simple numbers can lend some weight to a particular organization, it takes active followers to bring about achievement. Warm bodies aren't enough; people in motion, people in relationship—who are sold on an idea and brought into the common purpose—validate a project as something real to be reckoned with. Personal involvement doesn't ensure that the project is right or good or wise or well done, but it does create a need for others to address the effort, for those nearby—in other roles, on other teams or committees—to acknowledge and respond to this locus of activity.

The relationships surrounding Jesus of Nazareth are a common illustration of this follower contribution. For 30 years, Jesus was off the radar, living as an unknown in a backwater town. However, once 12 other people came alongside him, a movement was born—one that could not be ignored by either the religious or the political authorities of the day. One man's efforts might fizzle out, but a crowd attracts a crowd, and a dozen grew to a hundred and then thousands. Regardless of whether Jesus' words were accepted or believed, they demanded a response because other people began to listen and respond to them.

Through the contribution of credence, followers can shape the direction of a group's energy and perspective far beyond their own personal investment. It also means that we as followers can be the determining factor in seeing someone's vision become a reality.

Providing a Network of Support

When I first began to explore photography as a hobby, I was fascinated by spiders and their webs. Each evening in southern California, I would walk around the house, filling my camera's memory card with images of the webs that had been created that day. My front garden in the U.K. provides even more opportunities like this, since dozens of arachnids make their homes in the trees, plants, and bushes each autumn.

What is a spider without its web? No doubt you've found eight-legged creatures crawling up the walls of your home or between shrubs from time to time. Without a web, a spider is vulnerable, hungry, and out of place. Without the vibrating threads of its web to tip it off, it receives no warning of approaching danger; and it has no hope of catching lunch merely by scurrying over my wallpaper. It lacks much of the majesty and beauty of a properly situated spider, encircled by the wizardly geometry and engineering of its thread-web home.

The spider may be the architect, the primary weaver, the overseer, the resource manager, but the web plays a crucial role in the success of the spider's endeavors—even its survival. One of our opportunities as followers is to be part of a web, a network of support that contributes to the success of our leaders' efforts and brings about the achievement of our mutual aims and purposes.

Our contribution of support affects both our leader and our fellow followers. The spider has only a single web, but it is made of many strands. Those fibers are knit together, tied to one another, resulting in an intricate design of strength, resilience, and efficiency. Like strands of a web, we can work in harmony with our fellow followers, flexing as they flex, moving together in the winds of change, responding to the leader's needs. Good followership complements our co-laborers' efforts rather than competes against them.

Perhaps the analogy of the spiderweb is a bit uncomfortable. What if I said instead that we are all bananas? (Stay with me here!) I learned recently that a ripening banana is extremely powerful. Loads of unripe bananas are transported around the world in special containers, with great efforts taken to ensure that the fruit doesn't begin ripening too early and end up overripe for market. To bring the bananas out of dormancy, a currently ripening banana is added to the container. The chemical produced by the ripening banana triggers a response in the unripe ones, and they begin converting into tasty, nutritious food.

In our interactions with others, we have the opportunity to be a ripening banana. If we are moving forward in our journey toward health and wholeness, then we have the opportunity to contribute to the welfare of the rest of the bunch as well, to trigger in them—in an almost infectious way—similar movement toward improving their lives and followership. We can be a significant factor in creating an environment that fosters growth and productivity for our entire team or office. As we support our fellow followers, the whole effort benefits—our leader and ourselves as well—as we partner in the work.

How can we contribute to the support of our leader? Even though leaders do fill different roles than followers, we can aid leaders in their own roles and stewardship. Everyone, every leader, has finite capacity and a limited range of knowledge, abilities, and experience. As part of the network of support, we can help our leaders, whether by being available to provide perspective and affirmation, or by accepting an area of delegated responsibility to free up the leader's time.

> "Encouragement can and should move up the chain of command" (*Creative Followership*, 108).

We may look at the spider's web and observe, "Most of the time, the spider isn't doing anything. It just sits there!"—while the web undergoes constant tension to support the spider and survive the elements. We must protect ourselves from becoming jaded in offering our support. If I find myself receiving less encouragement and appreciation than I would like, it can be easy for me to retaliate—internally, at least—against my "do-nothing" boss. Don't let this temptation stifle your motivation to support your leader. Don't pull back on your own involvement because you want to force the leader to pull his or her "fair share." Don't sabotage the web just so that the spider has to remain active, scurrying about to repair breakages and to prevent things from slipping through the holes. Remember that if we want to follow well, we will avoid making some sort of passive-aggressive value judgment about our leader's diligence.

We are part of a community—likely several different communities. Not all of the relationships within those communities are peer-peer. We cannot simply ignore the facets of hierarchy that seem less appealing, such as having a boss. To do so harms the boss and the entire network. Instead, let us take our followership to a new level of service by taking our places in the intricate pattern and incredible construction of a web of mutual support.

Guiding from Behind

Being out in front is one of the holy grails of modern Western society. Much career rhetoric is dominated by the quest to be the one who is miles ahead of the rest. If we can get far enough ahead, our victory is assured. If we race ahead of everyone else, then we can be the first to cross the finish line, untouchable and unhindered by the other competitors.

But not every aspect of life is a competition. If the aim isn't to be the first to arrive at a destination, might it actually be harmful to create too much distance between ourselves and the pack?

You may have heard of the notion of leading from behind or leading up. I prefer to think of guiding from behind—not to indicate that followers can't or shouldn't lead, but to highlight the variety of roles needed to see a group move together to achieve its aim.

All groups need direction, and most groups need to be directed. The more people who get involved, the more important it is to have someone in front leading the way, establishing the path—someone who is familiar with (or at least clear on) the destination and who can help chart the way there. The group leader often fills this role. Whether holding up a brightly colored flag in a mob of tourists or being the first to step off the helicopter into hostile territory, the leader fulfills a vital need in enabling the group to get to where it wants to go.

However, blazing the trail is only one step in arriving at the destination. When walking as part of a group, I routinely fall to the end of the line. It's not because I'm slow or unfit (though both are slightly true), but rather I have a concern for making sure everyone gets to the destination. If I'm at the back, I can easily see if someone is wandering off course, if they stop for a break, or if some other unexpected event occurs. The rest of the group may continue on, but I can lend help if needed and keep everyone moving. Sometimes, it's little more than corralling companions, but at other times a significant need for rest or help may go unnoticed if the only one concerned with getting us to the goal is the leader who is at the very front of the line.

I learned this lesson, in part, through interactions with my wife. I tend to be a very focused shopper. I'm not one for browsing shelves or perusing windows. If I know where we're headed, I try and get there as quickly as possible. If my wife is even a half step behind me, she will likely stop to inspect something that catches her interest. Meanwhile, unaware, I continue walking. I may continue for several yards before I realize the person now a half step behind me is no longer my wife! She's still several yards back. I didn't know she had stopped, and so my leadership wasn't particularly helpful for getting her to the destination; I kept on going without realizing I was now walking alone. While it may sometimes be true to say "speed of the leader, speed of the team," it also happens that a fast leader may simply leave everyone else in the dust. This certainly doesn't help the group find its way forward, and it may create more work if the leader has to backtrack and invest more time and energy in restoring group cohesion.

At the end of the line, we can guide the "herd" from behind while keeping an eye on the leader, or at least on the aim and objective. We can guide our fellow followers and contribute to a higher degree of effectiveness by keeping everyone together, on the same page. If all followers act in this way, an incredible network of mutual support and concern develops; combining resources enables the entire team to move forward in unity.

I came across a simple but profound observation in exploring the nature of followership: "[Leaders] are sheep too."[1] Followers aren't the only ones who need guidance; my leader will also benefit from the perspective and influence that I can exert from behind.

There is a risk to being the leader, the person out front. There is no one to stop the first sheep from taking the fateful step over the cliff—unless another member of the flock knows the terrain or can see the hazard and raise the alarm before the leader takes a critical misstep.

In some situations, we may not be physically separated from our leader, but rather distanced by our individual perspectives and blind spots. It is impossible for one person to see all of the issues and to be aware of all the possibilities for danger or mistake. As we follow with excellence, we can offer our perspective to help our leaders as they endeavor to set the direction and pace for the group.

At times, this perspective may need to be constructively critical; it may be vital for us to recommend a course correction when the leader has moved off target, or when actual or potential problems have gone unnoticed. For a follower to remain silent at such a time could lead to a significant waste of resources or even more severe consequences. Of course, we should only offer such correction from the framework of honor and humility that we explored in the previous chapter; giving corrective feedback should not become a source of pride: "The ability to be able to see those problems is a cheap gift indeed."[2] Instead, we should take that awareness and use it to surmount real problems. From a proper place of relationship, this follower-given guidance becomes an incredibly valuable asset to the leader and the organization.

This guidance should extend to other concerns as well—not only about *where* we are going, but *how* we are getting there. Our leader may have a different perspective on matters of ethics and efficiency. Certainly, we all come with our own histories and cultures, which color our approach to achieving goals. Each leader will communicate and implement policies differently, and he or she is likely unaware of the wide range of alternate approaches. Here, too, the involved follower may be able to provide helpful perspective—not necessarily guiding the entire group, but by providing individual guidance to the leader concerning the most appropriate course of action.

However, guiding from behind is not merely offering perspective. It also means getting involved and doing the work. When I am behind and alongside my leader, I have the opportunity to contribute where my leader is lacking. As I observe and talk with my leader, I may discover places where I can fill in the gaps, offering strength where he or she displays weakness. In very tangible ways, I can help my leader excel in his or her role. It's important, though, to go about this type of service in a manner that doesn't humiliate our leaders. And we must avoid serving in a self-centered way, with an eye for currying special favor. If we can overcome these possible perversions, our guiding support can be very helpful indeed.

Developing Your Leader

From our obligation for personal development stems the opportunity to help our leaders to develop as well. Like followers, leaders can benefit from rightly offered perspective as they grow. This is where we as followers come in.

But before we go further, we must first wrestle with the idea of upward influence. Although shaping one's leader is an extension of the idea of influence that we discussed earlier, it is often a bit more sensitive.

Barbara Kellerman, who is an advocate of the validity of followership, made this definitive-sounding statement: "We must conclude, then, that however endearing the idea that subordinates can freely and easily impact on their superiors, it is mostly misguided."[3] We may assume that the nature of hierarchy—the stratification of leaders and followers—precludes any possibility for us becoming the kind of personal influence that would contribute to our leader's development. It may be that we cannot "freely and easily impact" those above us, but calling this contribution "misguided" is far from the truth. The degree of freedom and ease we encounter is determined by the dynamic of our follower-leader relationships.

As followers, we have plenty of opportunities to see our leaders' rough edges. We observe mistakes, perceive lapses in judgment, note errors in decision-making, cringe at word choice, and flinch at personality quirks. But while we may experience disappointment or frustration, what do we do with this burden of knowledge? Do we stockpile this ammunition for assaulting the leader's character and performance, or do we discover new frontiers where we can lend our abilities to enhancing the leader's contribution, character, and reputation?

Where we go from this place of perceiving "fault" in our leaders says a great deal about ourselves as followers. "The most capable followers in the world will fail if they gripe about their leaders but don't help them improve."[4] It doesn't take courage, wisdom, or healthy relationship to construct a list of someone's inadequacies. However, if we are to move from a place of resentment to one of support, we must have authentic concern and a healthy connection with our superiors. My leader will best receive my support if I have previously invested in establishing this rapport with her or him; I can then offer my perspective and suggestions from a well-developed foundation. How awkward (and ineffective) it would be to wait until the moment of criticism to first engage in this level of communication!

Perhaps our feelings of discontent are subtle and never spoken. "We privately complained, we may even have quit, but we rarely stepped forward to help them transcend their limitations and be the best boss they could be."[5] With such an attitude we forget to focus on improving the situation, with helping our boss; we end up dwelling on the perceived deficiencies rather than the person. This tendency can stem from our own ideas about leaders. For instance, if I imagine my leader to be the embodiment of superiority, then a misstep on his or her part will cause me to struggle with the resulting dissonance between my expectation and the reality. "Followers who expect their leader to have all the answers are naïve—and such expectations do their leaders no favors. The point, in an increasingly fast-changing and complex world, is to help leaders to learn."[6]

Our own feelings and responses as followers are only one side of the dynamic. The leader's attitude is also a critical factor in establishing an environment that permits this follower-based contribution to his or her personal development. Can we do anything to dictate to what degree our leaders are (or should be) open to such influence? We can engage in a real relationship with them, thus creating a mutual vulnerability and an avenue for encouragement.

Henry Ford said, "My best friend is the one who brings out the best in me." The answer to whether followers can have influence is, simply, yes—if I am intentional about being a true friend to my leader, caring about his or her success and excellence and health. If I desire to see my leader in a place that enables his or her best possible involvement, then I can make a significant contribution both to my organization and to my leader. But the starting place is relationship.

We must use well-founded relationships for encouragement: "Let leaders know we see their willingness to take on the challenge of transformation as a sign of their strength as a leader."[7] It is intimidating for anyone to admit personal faults, to acknowledge the need for change. For those who are looked up to, who are placed upon a pedestal of public opinion, the challenge is more difficult still. We cannot change our leaders, but we can encourage them in their personal development by praising the self-correction and growth we do see.

One of my leaders once told me that an invitation to leadership is a call to grow in public. Few of us followers have to deal with this challenging, trying aspect of leadership—although our own personal development may often become part of our public persona. Leaders will usually have many more eyes upon them than we have, and they will likely feel the weighty intimidation of knowing that they are under construction—they're not the finished article.

So what does effective encouragement look like? Pithy statements, anecdotes, and clichés—even if given with the best intentions—rarely provide the kind of impetus that a growing leader needs to confidently pursue personal growth: "For any encouragement to be effective, it must be specific, sincere, real, and truthful."[8] Some ideas for honest and effective encouragements include normalizing the journey ("I'm also trying to grow"), affirming the changes you see already, and helping the leader to envision the enhanced future that will result from his or her growth.

> "If we amplify our leaders' strengths and modulate their weaknesses, we are the gem cutters of leadership"
> (*The Courageous Follower*, 14)

Beyond attitude and encouragement, we can apply ourselves to the development of our leaders by stepping in and getting concretely involved in certain tasks. By doing so, we can free our leaders from some particularly time-draining burdens—ones that tend to rest on their areas of weakness rather than strength. By alleviating these burdens, we may not only help the organization as a whole, but also allow more space and resources for our leaders to grow.

I once had a team leader who had incredible strength and gifts in interpersonal relationships. A broad network of people around the world looked to him for friendship and input, and he also headed a particularly large team. While we team members each felt valued and connected, some aspects of team management were a stretch for our leader, calling for him to use resources that could be better spent elsewhere.

One of my teammates stepped in and offered to shoulder the burden of overseeing some of the team management tasks. His offer wasn't a value judgment ("you're really no good at this, so you should let me do it"), and it wasn't a play for personal power or an attempt to usurp authority. Rather, the offer was made so as to encourage our leader to focus on the tasks he was best at and to free up time, energy, mental space, and capacity so that he could invest in other areas, personally and on behalf of our team and organization.

For this arrangement to work, there had to be (and there was) a significant relationship between my teammate and the leader, and also between my teammate and the rest of our team. Such a delegation of authority required trust and authenticity, and the arrangement became a vital part of our team dynamic. This type of follower involvement encouraged our leader in his development, leading to an improved team experience for all of us—followers and leader alike.

7

OWNERSHIP: PASSION IN ACTION

I f we engage in work that we care about and are personally invested in, it becomes easier to fulfill our obligations and make
our best contributions in a life-giving, satisfying, and beneficial
way. When we do, we move beyond being a nameless cog in an
impersonal machine to becoming the actuation of something
deep within us. This sense of personal attachment to a project
or purpose can be captured in the term "ownership."

Moving from participation, to support, to ownership takes
us into a deeper level of contribution as followers, where we
can more fully use our abilities, offer our perspective, and exert
our influence. Whether we're concerned about the bottom line,
superior product quality, impeccable service, a successful char-
ity event, promoting a new policy, or increasing membership
numbers, acting from a place of ownership will release the best
of what we have to offer.

It's tempting to fixate on having a leadership role. Access to
that platform can seem like the key to fulfilling our goals. But it
is impossible for everyone to have a leadership position. Often a
group has only one person designated as leader—a person given
ultimate decision-making responsibility and authority. If attaining that leadership role were the only way we could fulfill

our passions and achieve our aims, then most of us would be doomed to disappointment.

However, while leadership titles may be limited, ownership is not; anyone can have a powerful sense of ownership. Any number of people can care about a project, demonstrate initiative, and personally feel the burden for seeing a vision realized. We can be a driving force and a critical factor—if we care to be.

> "[We are to] submit to authority, not to become a submissive person. There's a big difference between those two"
> (*I've Got Your Back*, 20).

Where do we begin? What is the foundation of ownership? It starts with our journey of personal development, which helps us to better know ourselves and clarify our vision. After we've worked on this, it becomes easier to name what it is that we truly care about—the goals, aims, and purposes that we have a deep-seated desire to fulfill.

Before laying this foundation, we may indeed voice concern about and perhaps even feel the weight of various ventures, but we would not have the deeply rooted sense of ownership that compels us to offer our very best. We can always choose to support and take responsibility for a vision for which we feel no sense of ownership, but in such cases we may lack the personal interest to see such a vision to its conclusion.

Although we don't necessarily need to feel ownership to make a productive contribution, a lack of ownership can be detrimental to a group's efforts. As one leader observes:

> One of the major issues I am struggling with in our area is a disconnect with my own leadership style and what I see as a "Gen Y" tendency in several of our team members to wait for the leader to tell them what to do. I have spent months trying various things to motivate them to be intentional and seek personal

vision, but I sense that several folks are just waiting for lightning to hit them or for me to give them specific ideas about what to do. As a result, we have not made much progress.

There may be some truth to this leader's perception of generational tendencies, but the more fundamental issue at hand is ownership. His team members did not have a clear sense of what they cared about; they had no personal investment in the work. Although they had ability and eagerness, they lacked an *internal* sense of direction and thus failed to recognize opportunities for involvement. As a result, a rather large group of people was looking to the leader to give them a sense of ownership; but ownership cannot be imparted. We can encourage and nurture it, empower and affirm it, but we cannot give someone else a sense of ownership—a motivating burden—for a particular work. The responsibility for embracing ownership lies with us.

Jef Williams, in his book *Leadership-Followership 360°*, outlines a variety of tasks for leaders. One is to "communicate the task," which he elaborates on, saying, "Communicate the ownership of the task. This means that the person assigned to the task will be ultimately responsible for its success."[1] While I would agree that delegating, communicating expectations, and outlining deliverables are essential aspects of good leadership, assigned ownership is weak in comparison to the internally acknowledged passion of ownership.

Rather than attempting to delegate ownership, a leader should communicate his or her concern for a particular project and ask whether others feel similarly about it. If there are at least some followers who do, then the leader can begin to tap into that resource, encouraging those who share a sense of ownership to personally and voluntarily buy-in to the idea or project. Sharing ownership for a goal has the added benefit of creating a significant partnership between the leader and followers as they build connections and cooperate.

As we intertwine our visions, our hopes, our hearts, perhaps even our finances with the fulfillment of some aim, we move from being participants to being fully invested partners, even if we may not have a formal leadership title to mark that reality. Rather than lemmings who march across the screen until they're told what to do, imagine a whole cast of characters who care intimately about a venture's outcome!

When we act from a place of ownership, we counteract some of the external misconceptions about followership. We as followers can be just as invested as any president, CEO, or chairman. We can be just as driven and passionate, just as concerned, just as excited as anyone else who may bear a more public position or formalized role.

But for our internal sense of ownership to have a positive (perhaps even corrective) effect, we must put it into action—as part of our excellent followership. Robert Kelley paints a picture of such engagement: It includes "taking joint 'ownership' of goal setting, group commitments, work activities, schedules, and group accomplishments. It also means being a positive contributor to the group's dynamics: helping everyone feel part of the team, dealing with conflict, and assisting others in solving problems."[2]

More than a simple to-do list, ownership provides us with a valuable compulsion to see an endeavor through to success. It takes us beyond our job description (in an appropriate way) to become a linchpin in a positive and effective community effort. Where questions of self-worth or lack of influence may threaten to discourage us, developing a sense of ownership can propel us forward with excitement.

We must develop ownership for ourselves. While the seeds of ownership may lie in the intrinsic wiring and vision of who we are, we shouldn't wait for a *feeling* of ownership to materialize. Sometimes we must simply jump in. Then the more we are involved, the more we care about the endeavor. The more we care about the endeavor, the stronger our sense of ownership and the greater our willingness to be more involved and to give more of ourselves. We benefit when we take ownership and allow it to drive our participation, stewardship, and support.

Not only does ownership encourage our excellent followership under a particular leader, it also enables the group's work to continue even in the wake of a leadership change. When followers care about and own a particular project, then even if the leader moves away, these followers can carry on the team's effort. History is replete with examples—everything from business ventures to religious cults—that fizzled away almost immediately after the founder moved, died, or got arrested. Such ventures are more personality cults than life-changing goals. If a broad base of ownership had existed, these efforts may still exist today.

My own study of leader-follower pairs from the Hebrew Bible (the Jewish Scriptures)—such as Joshua following Moses and Elisha following Elijah—highlights two common tendencies among followers with a sense of ownership.[3] First, these followers displayed an expressed desire not to leave or abandon their leader—far beyond a general commitment to the person.

> "The star follower always wants to be perceived as part of the community working within the framework, not an outsider trying to tear it down" (*How to Be a Star at Work*, 170).

Second, these followers showed an even deeper commitment to the cause; they faithfully continued the work even after the leader was gone. These followers did not necessarily seek the leadership position, but continued to operate from their sense of ownership, their passion and care for the vision. They felt empowered and responsible to maintain and expand on what their leaders had begun.

Good leaders who care about the organization's aims should encourage ownership as a powerful characteristic of excellent followership. We shouldn't assume that those who initiate a work will be around to see it through to completion. We cannot expect that the passion of a single leader will be sufficient to sustain a group for the long-term. We shouldn't trust that one person's charisma will be able to elicit the very best contribution from each member of the team. Ownership is a necessary resource.

Part 3

OBSTACLES AND
HOW TO OVERCOME THEM

We have already discussed inhibiting misconceptions about followership in Part 1, but there are other barriers to our followership that arise internally, relationally, and culturally—and must be overcome. These obstacles are not necessarily founded on errant thinking, but we must navigate them as part of the challenge of becoming an excellent follower.

8

INTERNAL CHALLENGES TO FOLLOWING WELL

However difficult the circumstances surrounding us, the factors that most seriously inhibit excellent followership arise from within us. We must make ourselves aware of these internal tensions so that we can successfully overcome them.

Originality

One night, when I was a teenager, I was out with two female friends and another guy. This guy was older than I was, and I had only just met him that night. Returning to the car in the parking lot, I noticed that the other guy was opening the door for the girl who was getting in on the driver's side of the vehicle. Not wanting to be upstaged by his exceptional attention to etiquette, I rushed over and opened the back door on my side of the car, trying to look like I was a sincere gentleman and not just a copycat. No one was fooled, and tension between the older guy and me persisted throughout the evening.

This episode was surprisingly profound for me. In that brief encounter, I saw the fullness of my own pride and jealousy—strong emotions that prevented me from being content to simply imitate and replicate something good. Rather than observing virtue in someone else and being moved to adopt a similar pattern in my own life, I found myself desperate to assert my originality and independence in acting chivalrous. Rather than accepting myself as a humble learner, happy to pick up on the good ideas and practices of others, I felt driven to display my innovation and trend-setting qualities. In the quest of displaying virtue, I actually undercut myself; my own twisted internal motivations perverted an opportunity to serve into a platform for competition and conflict.

Good followers know that other people are going to have original ideas, create processes first, and lead the way in initiating action. That's not to say that we won't have our own thoughts and vision, but it is more than likely that we won't be the first to do, say, or know something. If you, like me, have this internal desire to be an originator, a unique contributor, then this bent may prove to be a significant challenge.

Setting aside the desire to be the lone innovator requires humility and appreciation. Rather than seeing others as competitors—all of us vying to make our mark through foresight and creativity—we must grow to appreciate that our followership role often provides us with quality role models. We may work for or alongside those who have more experience or skill, or simply a different perspective, from which we can learn and glean valuable thoughts and habits.

If I believe that these nuggets of wisdom are worthless because I didn't think of them first, I miss out on one of the great benefits of working with others. If I let my lust for independence and uniqueness go unchecked, I miss these opportunities for

> "Exceed expectations even when no one is looking, even when there is a chance no one will know or understand what effort went into a task or project" (*Creative Followership*, 128).

positive growth and actually slip backward into a place of less health, wholeness, and effectiveness.

Ultimately, we must seek a balance: to offer our ideas and perspectives in good stewardship *without* coveting the suggestions made by others. We should freely express our creativity without succumbing to envy or jealousy when someone else's suggestion is better or voiced first.

Acknowledgment

Perhaps we struggle less with who acts first and more with who gets acknowledged. Many of us have a strong internal desire to be rewarded by receiving credit for our work. It can even feel unjust when someone overlooks our involvement. We want others to value us and our labor as much as—and even more than!—we do ourselves.

We all experience times when humility is foisted upon us. Sometimes we have no chance to advocate for the value of our participation, and others remain unaware of the difference we've made. I can think of any number of award ceremonies I've attended where individuals were called up on stage and thanked. My leg muscles twitched as I anticipated hearing my name next, then standing and walking to the stage to receive my applause and trophy. Yet my name was never called.

It's not unreasonable to expect to receive some affirmation and gratitude for our work. The challenge arises when credit and reward become the dominant motivation for following well. If this is the case, and we don't receive the recognition we yearn for, then the inspiration of reward inevitably gives way to poor internal—and external—responses. We must use self-discipline to constantly check the merit of our desires. As we make a presentation, as we write a memo, as we list contributors and make acknowledgments, are we framing things so that we receive primary credit for the effort, or are we content to share the spotlight—or perhaps even remain offstage entirely?

The devastating danger with this internal challenge is that when all of our team members strive for personal recognition, we are really no longer working together. We are viewing one another as competition, as if there is a finite amount of glory and thanks to go around and each of us wants to receive the largest share. Then we each begin to dance and manipulate, to spin truth and sugarcoat, trying to play to our personal advantage. We replace the heart of cooperation with a hunger for acknowledgment.

How do we prevent ourselves from slipping into this dysfunctional dynamic? We must consider our own desires, certainly. But we'll be even more effective if we intentionally offer thanks, praise, and rewards to others. Such effort has two benefits. First, it helps us to keep proper perspective about our own relative worth as a member of the group. We have not done it all on our own, and offering thanks to others reminds us that we are part of a larger community; each one of us adds his or her own time, energy, and thoughts to achieving our aims. Second, giving credit to others meets the needs of our coworkers who, like us, desire affirmation. If we offer this praise authentically and regularly, we'll feel a freedom emerge, reassurance that we don't have to force circumstances to gain the recognition that our ego needs. Instead, we'll experience contentment knowing that we, in turn, will not always be overlooked, that at least someone else out there sees us for who we are and values our involvement. We might not stand in the spotlight—but our coworkers' reflected attention may both motivate our work and keep us from unhealthy pride.

Risk

In contrast to desiring to boldly stand alone in the spotlight, the fear of taking risks can be an inhibitor to following well. We may hold back on offering our ideas and suggestions because we're not sure how well we'll be received. We risk being shut down by others or having our ideas judged as silly or unfeasible, overlooked or dismissed entirely. By offering input, we may even risk reprisal, discipline, or firing.

Risk is a reality. In every relationship, there is a certain amount of risk, and we're likely to feel this most acutely in the leader-follower dynamic. When we're keenly aware of our subordinate status, the temptation to clam up and hold back our ideas can be powerful. The fact that an entire book on this topic, *The Courageous Follower*, exists is testimony to the prevalence of risk in followership.

How do we deal with this particular challenge? We may take unhealthy approaches, like pretending that risk can be eliminated, or avoiding risks to the point of losing all opportunities for influence—and forfeiting our relationships as well. Pulling back does not nullify the reality of risk.

> "Good followership puts us at great personal risk ... it will also lead us into difficult places where we may not want to go. How tempting it is for us to choose neutrality, to stand by and do nothing" (*The Forgotten Art of Following*).

On the other hand, we may move into an aggressive mode, believing that presenting our opinions forcefully and frequently will somehow build up within and around us a tolerance to the effects of risk. We may hope that bravado and an air of invincibility will sway others away from challenging or censoring us. This approach, too, will likely lead to lost opportunities and relationships.

The best approach is to address risk from a place of healthy relationship. Regularly interact with both your superiors and your fellow followers, and keep lines of communication open so you are continually building a sizable deposit in the bank of trust. Then when confrontations, challenges, or disagreements arise, your relational resources will counter the risk. Our words and actions will still have consequences and repercussions, but each risk will be better addressed from the solid relational foundation you've created.

Although I am fairly risk-averse, I found myself much more willing to have a risky conversation with my previous team leaders—with whom I have long-standing friendships—rather than with leaders in a different segment of my organization whom I know only by reputation. Similarly, I am more prepared to have risky conversations with certain teammates than others because I have more history, connection, and understanding with them than with my newer teammates. It falls to me to intentionally cultivate the same kind of trust relationship with my newer coworkers so that, should the time come, there will be a healthy place for us to communicate ideas that might otherwise be prone to break down into miscommunication and hurt.

Again, we see that much of our excellent followership hinges on our attitude and relationships. Take time to cultivate both, for the benefit of yourself and your organization.

9

RELATIONAL CHALLENGES TO FOLLOWING WELL

No aspect of our followership journey is entirely individual. Every facet—from the misconceptions we encounter to our obligations and opportunities—takes place within relationship. Followership exists only within a relational framework: Someone else is a leader, and I am a follower. Excellent followership will never occur if we try to minimize or eliminate this reality.

I agree with this assertion about the modern working environment: "We face not the old dichotomies of tyranny versus freedom or individualism versus collectivism but rather a dichotomy of the sense of community versus the experience of estrangement."[1] We face the challenge of engaging in real relationships, of being followers from a true sense of community and connection with others, and not from a wounded or antagonistic place of isolation. Not surprisingly, then, communication issues, personality differences, and misaligned expectations can severely affect our excellence in followership.

As we interact with our leaders and fellow followers, we will inevitably face relational challenges. It's tempting to point fingers at others and dream of how things would be different "if only he or she would ... ." This attitude frees us from our own culpability in the matter, but such daydreaming rarely amounts to anything more than passive-aggressive backbiting, and it's never helpful. Rather than identifying and prescribing remedies for the faults we perceive in our leaders, we must improve the situation as a whole—which we can only do by being aware of where the challenges lie and managing our own perspectives and behaviors to promote the healthiest atmosphere possible for resolution and cooperation.

Communication

Relationships cannot exist without some degree of communication, even if it's infrequent or indirect. But communication is one of the primary challenges in working with others.

Finding my voice was one of the most difficult challenges I tackled in learning to relate well. Being relatively young and inexperienced—and serving in a role that didn't fit within the traditional leadership/career track of my organization—made it very difficult for me to know when and how to speak up. And many times, I didn't—which may have been the correct decision, but it also helped to establish others' perception that I didn't have much to contribute.

Leader-follower relationships are too varied to offer a one-size-fits-all approach to overcoming this challenge, but the first step is determining your own need to contribute. If you feel unimportant or undervalued, with no chance to offer your opinion, you must tell that to your superior. (A private conversation, before or after a larger-scale meeting, may be an appropriate time for such a talk.) Once you let your leader know of your desire to be involved, he or she may specifically solicit your perspective, overtly providing the okay for you to share input and thus removing some of your doubt or inhibition about expressing yourself. Or you may need to learn patience; it may take some time before you have earned the others' trust enough to be able to offer your thoughts publicly.

You may find, as I did, that being invited into a conversation by your leader is significantly freeing. When my leader asks for input, calling me out by name to share my thoughts, I know without a doubt that I am welcome to join in the dialogue. A leader who is unaware of your need to be encouraged, even prompted to share, may not naturally do so, which means that, not surprisingly, the remedy to this communication challenge lies in *communicating*.

Even so, sometimes the sequence of communication can be a challenge. Am I only allowed to share my thoughts after a decision has been made? Do others get the first or last word, and if so, does that invalidate my contribution? I have worked with a number of leaders who intend to communicate a proposition, but their words come across as if they are stating a fact—merely informing us of something that's already been finalized.

> "It is up to followers to be clear about the value they place on consultation and participation"
> (*The Courageous Follower*, 94).

Here, again, the solution begins with self-awareness about the kind of contribution you need—and feel qualified—to make. I found that I resented not being included in decisions that would ultimately affect my responsibilities. In part, I felt ignored or overlooked—didn't they know that their decision affected me?—but I also realized that without my added viewpoint, the decision would not be as well-founded. Visionaries making systems-based decisions may inherently overlook or undervalue the perspectives of those with different abilities and experiences—invaluable input for bringing about the best decision possible.

On the other hand, there were other decisions and conversations that I felt perfectly happy to be excluded from, times I felt that I didn't have much to offer. We help ourselves when we learn to identify when we should speak up. And when we don't have the opportunity to speak, even if we would like to, then we need to refer back to our obligations as followers to honor and submit. When we consider our communication needs and share those expectations—whatever the outcome is—we take a step forward in following with excellence.

Personality Differences

We are individuals; we each think, speak, and act differently than those around us. But others' values, experiences (positive and negative), and motivations, though distinct from our own, are no less valid or significant. When such dissimilarities arise—where no one is right or wrong—we may feel the clash of personality differences, as perceived incompatibilities rub up against one another and neither side seems to give way.

For example, I struggle with following well under any leader whom I perceive to be territorial, defensive, prideful, or fearful. But it is possible that my perception is not reality. What I see as territorialism may actually be a leader's strong sense of responsibility over a project. What I see as defensiveness may stem from the high degree of personal investment a leader has made in a particular venture. What I label as pride may be colored by my own jealousy and envy. What I consider fear may be prudent hesitation or caution. Of course, my perceptions could be correct, but it's my responsibility to consider the motivations that may lie under the surface. Is my leader actually a selfish jerk, or does he or she see important values that I am unaware of—and does he or she simply struggle to communicate those well?

Pacing is another quality that may challenge your followership. We're not talking about meandering up and down hallways (though you're sure to be challenged by your leader if you make a habit of this!) but about a leader's sense of how quickly or slowly to make decisions and take action. If your leader's natural bent is to move faster or slower than you are inclined to do, you will inevitably feel some tension. You may feel that you have an unrelenting slave driver for a supervisor or that you are being unfairly reined in when you have so much to contribute.

Remember that trust creates the foundation that allows us to remain open to different possibilities and explanations— ones that don't naturally occur to us. Do we trust our leaders' ultimate motivations? Do we trust their abilities? Do we trust their intentions?

What do we do when we believe in our leaders' goals and aims, but we're unsure of their character or methods? We continue to faithfully fulfill our obligations while looking for opportunities to contribute. We acknowledge a degree of latitude in valid approaches. We don't allow such differences to become divisive, breaking down our leader-follower relationship and restricting our ability to follow with excellence. To reiterate, it is not for us to simply wish that our leaders would change to alleviate tension, but rather to remain aware of our own motivations, to continue in our journey of personal development, and to commit to establishing an environment and relational dynamic that will enable each person involved to make his or her very best contribution to the group's purpose.

Expectations

When consulting with teams about effective cooperation, I most commonly start by encouraging them to identify and communicate their expectations. Misaligned and unspoken expectations are some of the most destructive sources of tension any relationship will face.

We must become aware of the variety of sources that shape our expectations before we'll ever be able to articulate them. We have expectations for ourselves, for our leaders, for our peers. Our peers have expectations for us and for our leader. Our leader has expectations for us and for our peers. Others— stockholders, donors, team members, other teams—also have expectations for us, our peers, and our leaders, both individually and collectively. And the organization as a whole, with its core values and history, will have expectations for how we pursue our work. Expectations form a complicated web of vested interests, hopes, dependencies, promises, contracts, commitments, agreements, emotions, traditions, deadlines, and codes of conduct.

How can we possibly avoid utter dysfunction when working within such a complicated network, in which each person has opinions about what every other person is doing and how? Again, communication is key. We must communicate as many of our own expectations as possible—not necessarily with the hope that all our expectations will be met, but rather in an effort to declaw the possibility that misaligned expectations will disrupt communication on a regular basis. To communicate our expectations, we must first identify our needs. In this process, it can be helpful to imagine situations we may not yet have faced, and anticipate what our views might be. The more that we can proactively unearth these expectations— rather than waiting for them to suddenly manifest in the midst of a crisis—the better our chances for maintaining excellence in our followership, and the less likely we'll be to make demands, decry unfairness, or feel wounded.

> "We must develop a culture of openness in which leader, followers, and peers make themselves vulnerable to one another"
>
> (*Reworking Authority*, 27)

Do you expect that your leader wants to lead? When you join a team, a club, or a department, do you presume that the person in charge has that role because he or she wants it? Do you jump to the conclusion that his or her ideal role includes having responsibility for the organization or the project?

I have often seen—in education, volunteer organizations, and even in businesses—that the person with the desk, keys, corner office, or name on the letterhead is not always excited about that role. If I expect that every leader wants to lead, then I may be baffled when I encounter leaders who are worn out, discouraged, uncertain, struggling with inadequacy, or dissatisfied. After all, don't they enjoy all the perks that come with their role? Aren't they thankful to have this elevated position? Don't they relish the power, responsibility, and resources that accompany their job?

The way to correct this misperception (as with most other interpersonal challenges) is to build a healthy relationship with your leader. Get to know her or him as an individual. Build trust. Evaluate your presuppositions and expectations. Likewise, get to know yourself and learn to easily communicate your values to others. By doing so, you'll get to know others too—and from this place of understanding springs encouragement for others and excellence within yourself.

10

CULTURAL CHALLENGES TO FOLLOWING WELL

In addition to our attitudes and the influence of our immediate relationships, our excellence in following may be impeded by the values and mechanisms ingrained in our structures, language, and nation.

It is vital for us to resist decrying all cultural differences as wrong or evil, to resist the influence of prejudice and stereotyping when considering our participation and interaction within a group dynamic. Whether we are working within our own culture or alongside and within a culture that is foreign to us, we must be aware of cultural challenges and make an ongoing commitment to personal growth and humility to successfully navigate and follow with excellence amid the various differences.

Some approach this challenge by poring over lists of characteristics that define and distinguish one particular culture from another—and there is certainly value in having a base level of knowledge from which to operate. But ultimately we relate to people and not to entire nations painted with strokes so broad that they are, at best, only partially or occasionally true.

We would all do well to consider the perspective for developing appropriate responses to culture as presented in the book *Cultural Intelligence*: "The essence of culture is subtler [than laundry lists of characteristics], it is expressed in combination with the unique personality of each individual, and it is hard to express in print. Formal and abstract knowledge needs to be supplemented by and integrated with experience of the culture and interactions with its people. Learning facts about other cultures is not enough."[1]

When our goal is to relate to people, it helps to consider various paradigms for cultural understanding and surface some aspects of organizational involvement that may prove especially challenging to excellent followership. In our exploration of culture's affect on followership, we consider not only national and ethnic cultures, but corporate cultures as well.

Structure

Organizational structures do exist (and we've already explored the reality that hierarchy does not inherently detract from achieving a group goal or following with excellence). However, the particular structure within which we serve can still present difficulties for us in fulfilling our followership roles.

Many organizations have communication protocols—"chains of command," either formal or implied, about who can speak with whom about what. Even within the flattest of hierarchies, marked lines and boundaries exist between departments and teams, and crossing those lines to speak with superiors may be considered inappropriate.

Does your organization's structure permit this kind of communication? Are you free to confront your leader about an issue or concern? Is it taboo to speak to your leader's leader, or the leader of a different department or team? Where can you go to lodge complaints or criticism? If you have a concern related to your direct leader, is there a way for you to appropriately share this perspective with someone in the hierarchical structure?

I have often heard of or even borne witness to team members who have sent an account of perceived injustice to the person with the highest level of leadership for whom they could get an email address. Having worked with their leader, and their leader's supervisor—still without achieving the desired outcome—they kept going up and up. We might admire their tenacity to fight for what they believe in. But unfortunately, even within an organization with a rather small degree of "power distance," repeated efforts to leap up the chain of communication often come across as immature, inappropriate, and insubordinate.

> "The best structure at a given moment depends primarily on the availability of suitable people" (*Cultures and Organizations*, 230).

The notion of "power distance" describes one facet of national and organizational culture that can help us understand the kinds of interactions we may witness. Articulated by Geert Hofstede as part of his multi-dimensional evaluation of cultures,[2] and explored by Gene Boccialetti under slightly different headings, "power distance" is the degree to which members expect or accept power to be distributed unequally. High power distance connotes ready acceptance of hierarchy where power is not shared equally among all members, where there are noticeable differences between levels of leadership and general membership. Low power distance refers to much more egalitarian approaches. Neither end of the spectrum is right or better; they are simply varying ways that communities and societies choose to function.

As Hofstede notes, "Power distance ... derives its name from ... the emotional distance that separates subordinates from their bosses."[3] Thus, at its heart, this national characteristic reveals facets of interpersonal relationship—the structures that arise tend to reflect the kinds of relationships that people expect. To navigate organizational structures is to navigate relationships.

More specifically, Hofstede asserts that power distance is about "dependence relationships," the degree of engagement and amount of access desired between authority figures and followers. When power distance is small, there is a high degree of interdependence and consultation between followers and leaders; they work closely and directly with one another.[4] This degree of interdependence is such that, "In the small power distance situation ... the hierarchical system is just an inequality of roles, established for convenience; and roles may be changed."[5] Here, we may expect a fluidity of structure, as the need for particular kinds of interaction may change and the structure morphs to accommodate and promote these interactions.

In contrast, where large power distance exists, we may expect less flexibility and movement within the structure. Hofstede notes that size of population is one of the primary predictors of the amount of power distance; large populations generally correspond to large power distance. In such situations, large nations or organizations tend to expect more distance and more non-participatory dependence, rather than cooperative interdependence, on authority figures simply because those in power are less accessible to the masses.[6]

Keeping power distance in mind, let's consider our desires for involvement and our hopes for working closely with our superiors. If we prefer an environment with a small power distance, but find ourselves within a large power distance culture, we may be frustrated at what we perceive as limitations on our access to those in leadership. We may feel unimportant or undervalued when it seems that our contribution is not needed or welcomed by those operating in other strata of the organization.

Conversely, if we prefer large power distance and the surrounding structure embodies a small degree of power distance, we may feel unnecessarily bothered by our leaders when they seem to be overtly guiding us or looking over our shoulder while we work. We may dismiss such leaders as incompetent, apparently unable to make decisions on their own and without our input. We may further feel that our time is being wasted by being brought into discussions that are irrelevant to us or that distract us from carrying out our own tasks.

For those who prefer a large power distance orientation, the experience of small power distance may actually feel risky. Ambiguity about who's in control and where the expertise lies can lead to uncertainty about what will happen when crises or difficulties arise. Clear hierarchy can be a relief—and an assurance that subordinates will be appropriately protected and cared for by competent leaders who can stand on their own.[7] In either case, we'll face challenges if our personal preferences don't align with our organization's structure.

Practically speaking, it's important for us to recognize that there are indeed norms and expectations about behavior within the structure. Perhaps sending emails and cc'ing your leader is fine, but face-to-face meetings with certain superiors are perceived as inappropriately formal. Maybe private communication is completely acceptable, but public criticism or disagreement is not tolerated. Figure out these organizational policies and preferences and be intentional about how you communicate within them. Carefully weigh whether violating these expectations is worthwhile, and whether it is even an effective way to pursue your aims.

Ira Chaleff makes a helpful distinction between hierarchical structure and hierarchical relationships.[8] With hierarchical structure, a pattern of governance and responsibility should prevent total chaos and unrelenting conflict. Having someone who is empowered to give the final decision in the midst of dilemmas should prevent a total collapse of this pool of human resources. Of course, such empowerment can be abused or neglected, but some amount of organization seems to be a positive quality.

Hierarchical relationships, on the other hand, must be handled much more cautiously. Some distinction between leader and follower roles is real and appropriate, but the separation between the roles can inhibit collaboration rather than enhance it. If distance prevents the flow of communication—such that subordinates are either intimidated or forbidden from providing information to superiors—then common aims will suffer. If followers perceive that leaders operate in some other world, far removed from the followers' realities, then they are far more likely to discredit or refuse decisions made by these authority figures.

It's rare to find a new employee orientation that includes an explanation of a company's hierarchical dynamics, in part, because such realities are difficult to articulate. As followers, we can help ourselves and our peers by asking questions and proactively trying to discover these expectations before stumbling into them. Using some of the tools discussed in the next chapter can help us gain an awareness of the preferences that may exist, and guide our investigation into the hierarchies of our working relationships.

Labels

Words matter. The terminology we use to describe things communicates much more than the formal definition attached to any given word. Within and across cultures, we use certain terms differently—the same words can have different connotations depending on the context. If a discussion includes words that communicate poorly or touch on personal sensibilities, then this facet of culture can inhibit the effectiveness of our working environment.

> "Followers have to overcome considerable social conventions to challenge the leader's position" (*Power of Followership*, 170).

Within your area of involvement, what is your personal list of "bad words"? Which terms cause you to cringe, to become defensive, to disengage? Which expressions make you think

I wouldn't have said it that way? How do you explain your role in ways that communicate value to you? Are you a volunteer? Employee? Partner? Member? Teammate? What words can your leaders use that don't cause you to question their intentions?

Now let's turn things around. How do you think your leader feels about certain terms? When you refer to your director as "boss," is that welcomed language or does it create a sense of separation or formality that your leader is uncomfortable with? When you address the committee chair as "Chairwoman Rodriguez," does she appreciate the title of respect or does she perceive some degree of antagonism or opposition as a result?

We should pay attention to individuals' preferences and norms within our organizations when we consider our language and the labels we use. Since the history and foundation of an organization define its culture and shape the approved avenues of communication, coming into such an environment can be challenging if the accepted labels and categories are left unexplained.

I recall struggling when my leader gave me the opportunity to offer input into the creation of my own job description and title. Very few others had the same role in the organization as I did, so there was little in the way of standards to guide me. I didn't know how to label my role: Administrator? Associate? Executive Assistant? What term would accurately communicate to others the nature of my role while also giving me the freedom to fully engage in my work?

Later, I was part of an extremely effective virtual team. Our six members were spread across four countries, and no one formally served as the group's leader. More than once, someone outside the group tried to pin us down: Who's leading this thing? Is it you? The reality was that denoting a leader would not have been helpful to us. We didn't need that label. Thankfully, we had the freedom—as well as a healthy relational foundation—to organize ourselves and still operate effectively.

In both of these experiences, self-awareness, relationships, and communication led me through the challenge of labels. I settled on an appropriate and accurate job title, and later felt fine avoiding the declaration of a formal leader for the group.

However, we won't always have the opportunity to use only language we're most comfortable with; our organization's structure may simply not allow it. In these times, we must be willing to adapt our jargon so we can effectively communicate to others and also speak up when their word choice is especially difficult for us to accept.

One of the most valuable pursuits any group can undertake is to build a common vocabulary. Identify what words you'll use and how you'll use them—casting off any ambiguity or suspicion that may be related to meaning or value. If you and your team can agree on categories and paradigms, if you highlight those areas where precision in communication is necessary and important, if you have the freedom to seek clarification and to voice discomfort about certain terms, you'll benefit from an open and empowering work environment.

Cross-Cultural Differences

Even the most similar people are different in some regard. The language we use, the things we value, the perspectives we cling to, the traditions we uphold, the way we navigate various relationships—toward superiors, peers, and subordinates, toward the elderly or the young—will differ even among people from relatively similar backgrounds. My wife and I have much in common: We both hail from coastal states in the U.S., are similar in age, have the same Myers-Briggs type preferences (see next chapter), and were raised in Christian homes in suburbia. Despite our high degree of similarity on paper, we quickly discovered that we had very different ideas about how best to organize our lives, how to make use of our free time, and what the distinctions are between "tidiness" and "cleanliness."

We discovered profound differences that affect our "working relationship" even though much of our culture is shared.

Many of these differences—personality, habit, preferences—become all the more volatile when we find ourselves working with or alongside people who have a different cultural background than we do. Add to this the significance of communicating across cultures—even among people who speak the same language (just ask my British friends and "neighbours")—and it's readily apparent that, to follow with excellence, we must address the ramifications of our culturally derived differences.

The global community and mobility of society ensure that, wherever we are involved, we are likely to encounter someone of a different culture or subculture. Despite the ease of worldwide communication, however, culture is just as significant as ever in shaping our identity and personhood. Larry Hirschhorn notes, "One's profession, one's employer, and one's residence are eroding as signs of one's identity. This is one reason why people have, increasingly, sought solace as well as inspiration in their ethnic or religious identities."[9] As a result, our journey of following well necessitates that we consider cross-cultural factors as part of the array of challenges we may face.

> "An obvious question…concerns how cultural values, such as individualism and collectivism, may affect [followership]"
> ("The Emergence of Implicit Followership Theory," 7).

I use the word "cross-cultural" to refer to interactions involving people representing distinct national, ethnic, and/or linguistic backgrounds. Cross-cultural relationships may involve a person living and working outside of their homeland, or a person or small group existing as a minority in an organization where most of the other members represent a different culture. It may even be that two or more people from different places

find themselves working together within a third cultural environment—which could be a different country or an organization that has a strong majority sharing some ethnic or linguistic
identity. Think of a Hong Kong businessman in Seattle. Or an
American teacher working at a school in Brazil. Or a mixed
team of British and Australian citizens providing disaster relief
in Japan. This is our modern reality: "Globalization affects not
only businesses and their managers but employees at all levels,
as well as customers and indeed everyone in the general population. Inevitably, globalization brings about interactions and
relationships between people who are culturally different."[10]
Cross-cultural considerations are not just for leaders—they are
relevant to followers as well.

Although relationships are between people, not geopolitical
entities, our culture of origin and/or the culture within which
we work have a profound effect on our thinking, speaking, and
actions. Cultural norms affect nearly every aspect of life, and
while individuals routinely deviate from their culture's standards, that culture's influence is often so intrinsic and subtle
that we may not be aware of how it is shaping the nature of our
followership. We must pay attention to the threads of culture
woven into each of us, and into our interactions, or we run
the risk of utter confusion. As we attempt to identify some of
the areas where special consideration of cross-cultural factors is warranted, our goal is to understand our relationships
with others, to engage appropriately with them, and to fulfill
our followership role in a way that will be well-intentioned,
well-executed, *and* well-received no matter the mix of cultures,
perspectives, and expectations.

Cross-culturally, communication is a complex endeavor and
there is every possibility for misunderstanding and even offense.
Body language and words may all carry different meaning even
when outwardly appearing the same. Holding up two fingers in
the U.S. may stand for the number two; in the U.K., it's a vulgar
gesture or a peace sign, depending on which way your hand is

turned. Words such as "pants," "boot," and "hole-in-the-wall" all carry different meaning on either side of the Atlantic. (In Britain, "pants" are underwear, a "boot" is the trunk of a car, and a "hole-in-the-wall" is an ATM, while in America, they are trousers, footwear, and a very small shop or restaurant.) A British friend of mine likes to joke that Americans and Brits are two peoples separated by a common language.

Consider, then, when there isn't a common language or when there are vastly different levels of fluency. Communication becomes more challenging, but no less vital. Even basic engagement can bring the relationship to a stalemate. (I recall a humiliating experience during my time living in the Middle East. I tried to buy a loaf of bread, but because I did not understand the price, I could only stare dumbfounded at the shopkeeper, with my palm full of coins.) Then consider the difficulty in relating more abstract ideas—your thoughts, feelings, and expectations. Intention, effort, and patience in learning to communicate are essential for everyone who wants to follow well. Unfortunately, the effort required can deter us from working hard to engage deeply with our fellow followers and leaders within a cross-cultural dynamic. Authors David Thomas and Kerr Inkson include giving up as one of many intercultural failures that is all too common today.[11] An unwillingness to do the work of learning to communicate will guarantee a severe limitation on excellent followership for those of us with any degree of cross-cultural engagement (which is likely most of us).

By some estimates, there are approximately 16,000 ethnic groups on our planet.[12] I, of course, can't cover even a fraction of the ways in which the combination of cultures represented in a leader-follower dynamic may affect your followership and your relationships. But I can encourage you to seek an awareness that enables you to proactively navigate the differences. Some of the resources discussed in the next chapter will be useful to that end, but there are a few perspectives that can help us from the outset.

For example, Hofstede describes another dimension of culture in the spectrum of individualism and collectivism. Although some consider this to be the most useful facet of culture to consider,[13] I agree with Hofstede's own assessment that it is one piece of a much larger picture, and that this dimension works in tandem with others (such as power distance).[14]

Briefly,[15] individualist cultures tend to be characterized by expressing values related to loosely knit connections with others, personal time, freedom, challenge, employee independence from the organization, telling the truth, and the management of individuals rather than units, teams, departments, etc.

On the other hand, collectivist societies will value tightly knit groups, training, organizations providing for employees and creating a dependent relationship, discouraging direct confrontation and the expression of personal opinions as subversive of the group's needs. Collectivist cultures tend to be externally shame-based rather than internally guilt-oriented. Collectivist relationships emphasize the importance of establishing trust before engaging in business, while regarding such relationships as a moral good rather than a calculated transaction. There are certainly relationships and groups to be found within both types of cultures, but "collectivists actually tend to have fewer groups with which they identify, but these are wide, diverse groups ... and the bonds of loyalty are strong. Individualists often identify with many different groups, but the bonds are superficial."[16]

> "Leadership/followership theorists should be careful not to presume that all cultures can function on a western contrived model" ("Comparing Followership with Servant Leadership," 16).

Although many prominent Western nations exhibit an individualist bent, Hofstede's research reveals that only a minority of people actually live in individualist societies.[17] Thus those of us from a Western, individualist culture must be careful about how we foist our expectations and values upon others. We must be mindful that, although we may have a dominant voice or influence in some circumstances, we may actually represent a minority perspective and we're certainly not always right.

We can easily create value-laden generalizations and stereotypes when working with someone who represents a culture different from our own. We may find it hard to affirm the neutral nature of our differences, preferring instead to resort to categories of right, wrong, or inappropriate. We may judge and criticize before even getting to know our leader or peers as people, painting them solely with our perceptions of their national or cultural identity. Such generalizations "conceal huge variances within that country and considerable subtlety in the way cultural differences are made apparent."[18] Even worse, we may use culture to try to erase the individuality of the people we are working with. As Geert Hofstede, a pioneer of evaluating cross-cultural interaction, reminds us, "Culture should be distinguished from human nature on one side, and from an individual's personality on the other."[19] We must remember that while there are differences between people of even the most similar backgrounds, there are also commonalities that unite us all as human beings. When we come across culture and personality differences and cannot legitimately say that someone is incorrect in their approach, we should persist in finding resolution amid conflicting perspectives.

Remember that one of our obligations as followers is submission. This obligation usually surfaces in the realm of decision-making. Thomas and Inkson say it well: "Decisions are affected by the motives and goals of those who make them ... [and] motives vary with culture."[20]

We'll have more to explore about motives when we discuss clarifying vision (Chapter 12), but here I'll simply say that individualists tend to be concerned with the content of a decision while collectivists tend to question how the decision is made

and who makes it.[21] Despite these differences, there are universal human concerns, basic problems worldwide regarding
relation to authority, conception of self (the dynamic between
an individual and the society), and dealing with conflicts.[22]
All people will feel the weight of these issues and seek to address
them, albeit with different approaches. When our approaches
to life, relationships, and cooperation feel vastly different from
one another, we have the opportunity to step back and find
common ground.

Rather than coming in with judgment about peculiarities of
language, activity, social etiquette, character, or competence,
offer humble curiosity. From the posture of a learner, ask what,
why, and how. Instead of presuming that your perspective or
approach is superior simply because it seems most sensible to
you, remember that you have much to gain by way of understanding and trust when you suspend your inner drive to create
conformity and instead seek an authentic experience of the
other person's perspective.

In addition, consider whether you are a member of the
host/majority culture of your organization, or whether you
are a guest/minority member serving within a culture that is
not your own. If you are a member of the local or predominant
culture and your leader is of a different nationality or ethnic-
ity, you may find that the nature of your followership skews
toward disempowering and discouraging your leader. You may
frequently offer correction or criticism, implying *that's not
how we do things here*, and reinterpret or dismiss your leader's
communication. Such actions will significantly erode his or her
likelihood of success. The repeated use of "we-you" language
reinforces differences and continually undercuts any possibility of deep unity and cooperation.

If instead you are working, volunteering, or otherwise operating across cultures and under the leadership of someone of a
different culture, appropriate submission becomes all the more
important. Even if you were invited as an expert or honored

guest, exercise caution in the language you use and the presumptions you exhibit. In some cultures, your uniqueness may ascribe special influence to your words and behavior, and you may unwittingly or unintentionally shame or disempower the local leader by breaking from cultural etiquette. As followers, we must be committed to honoring our leaders, even when we do not fully understand all of their words and expectations.

How can we avoid causing offense? How can we hope to navigate the untold number of discrepancies between cultures? Ask. If you are unsure of how to respond or speak to a leader or a fellow follower of another culture, ask him or her what would be appropriate. When facing a new situation or communicating about something sensitive, be cautious with your language. Preface your remarks by stating your intent and asking how your words or actions come across. This gives you the opportunity to correct any misunderstanding or judgment by reinforcing what you actually mean rather than igniting unknown cultural perspectives that would interpret your behavior in unintended ways.

While it takes courage, time, and energy (and perhaps some foreign language ability) to ask such questions, I have found that most people appreciate the question rather than the presumption. The dictum "it's easier to ask forgiveness than permission" does not apply in most cross-cultural interactions. If the goal is to establish relationship, it's far better to begin by voicing uncertainty and seeking clarity. That way, you can avoid needing to repair the damage of offensive speech or humiliating actions—especially since that reconciliation needs to take place within the same cross-cultural relationship that was broken by the original presumptions!

Certainly, the language used and the successful fulfillment of expectations may look different for leaders of another culture, so it is best to ask what he or she thinks of your followership. When we use an awareness of culture to explore how we can participate, steward, honor, and submit, we vastly improve the likelihood that our efforts will be well-received by our superiors and colleagues.

Remember that cultural differences can be expressed both in values and in practices. At times, people may do different things for the same reasons, with the same motivation, intent, and underlying values. At other times, people may engage in externally identical actions fueled by very different perspectives and visions.

Imagine two people both schedule a team calendar review meeting—one of them motivated by a desire to clarify all administrative details, the other interested in the relational aspects of who will be out of the office and whether some team members are traveling too frequently. Even though the outward action is the same, the differing motivations will surface in the great disparity of questions that will be asked, the tone of the meeting, and the nature of what's captured in the meeting's minutes. On the other hand, you may have witnessed two people both concerned with resolving a conflict. The same motivation may lead to different actions as one person takes the approach of scheduling a one-on-one lunch meeting while the other sends out a group email.

The different approaches taken in these scenarios are not right or wrong. But rather than assuming you know someone's motivations or goal, ask. Asking, with the goal of learning, is our best hope for overcoming cross-cultural challenges. As I've said before, we do ultimately relate to individuals (or is this merely my own individualist perspective?), but culture plays a significant role in shaping our actions and values. To ignore its influence is to almost ensure misunderstanding and miscommunication.

Adopting the posture of learner will allow you to follow well in a cross-cultural situation, but it will require time and patience. Working with peers from other cultures may be frustrating. You may be tempted to decry the "waste" of energy spent on sorting through the cross-cultural working dynamic, resources that could be otherwise focused on more directly achieving the organization's larger aims. On the other hand, the challenge of cross-cultural cooperation may feel too complex to untangle—and seem largely unimportant considering the "hopelessly" insurmountable interpersonal differences.

While the organization's aim and our common purpose are significant aspects of what binds us together in our followership roles, we must realize that excellent followership entails more than merely achieving results and attaining goals. The process of how the vision is realized is also important. Steamrolling our leader or our peers, even if doing so fulfills our organization's aims, does not mean we're successful followers.

Our goal is not mere productivity. Our goal is to faithfully fulfill our role of followership. We must navigate the many challenges presented by people and relationships—challenges that we face internally and externally, individual barriers along with communal and cultural hardships—and navigate them responsibly if we are to maximize all that our follower role can be.

11

RESOURCES FOR PERSONAL DEVELOPMENT

A primary aspect of personal development is self-awareness. I'm not talking about some sort of meditative self-consciousness, but rather an accurate sense of who you are, what makes you the unique person you are at present and that you may grow to become. The simple heading of self-awareness covers a broad spectrum: personality, preferences, values, strengths, weaknesses, talents, experiences, beliefs, relational wounds, emotional baggage, temptations, coping mechanisms, stress responses, communication patterns, interpersonal needs, and more.

I encourage you not to try to decipher or decode others, but to develop an understanding of yourself within the specific environment of interaction, communication, and relationship with a particular person (perhaps of another culture). In considering personal development and growing self-awareness, the goal is not to erase ourselves so that we might be more acceptable to others. Rather, we are pursuing a place of health from which our thoughts and actions can emerge as a help and not a hindrance to our followership.

David Thomas and Kerr Inkson describe this pursuit as *mind-fulness*, which they define as "the ability to pay attention in a reflective and creative way to cues in the cross-cultural situations encountered and to one's own knowledge and feelings."[1] We are not trading our culture or personality for someone else's; we are coming to know ourselves better, both within our own culture and in interactions with others. Mindfulness "does not mean abandoning who we are but rather using attention to become aware of differences and to think differently."[2]

Truly, we are complex beings, and no single tool can accurately summarize all the nuances of who we are. However, bit by bit, we can gain clarity on the depths of our individuality and relationships. We can also grow in our ability to articulate these things to others and to lay out pathways for our personal growth. As we identify accurate descriptions of ourselves and surface the "rough spots" in our character, we will be making best use of the resources mentioned below.

Although many books reserve their recommended resources for the final chapter or appendix, holding off until the very end to interact with some valuable tools runs contrary to my main hope that we will all find the support, vision, and perspective that we need to follow well. Most of the resources here focus on helping in the areas of personal development and relationship building, and they are, in my opinion and experience, a critical component in faithfully fulfilling our followership roles.

> "Creative Followership is about shaping your character"
> (*Creative Followership*, 21).

MBTI®

The Myers-Briggs Type Indicator® (MBTI®) is a well-established tool with a broad and deep research background. Its purpose is to assist users in identifying which one of 16 types best describes them in terms of how they go about life and how they see the world around them. All 16 types—each represented by a four-letter code such as ISTJ or ENFP—are presented positively; one type is not better than another or more suited to a particular role. Rather, each type describes a particular wiring, giving attention to how a person with such wiring might prioritize (and excel at) various mental functions.

The amount of research behind the MBTI® makes it a valuable paradigm for exploring topics such as how you communicate, how you respond to leadership, and how you deal with conflict. In my experience, the MBTI® has proven especially helpful in validating interpersonal differences, while surfacing my own tendencies and potential shortcomings. For example, my MBTI® results prompted me to explore how my personality type tends to deal negatively with prolonged seasons of stress. This helped explain the cause behind some very negative reactions I was having within a particular team situation. Once I was able to own the reality of my situation (and my accompanying response), I could move forward with my team into a much greater place of health and understanding.

While the MBTI® has been helpful in guiding my own personal development, I also find it useful for pinpointing how I differ from my coworkers, and consequently how best to capitalize on our preferences and strengths as a group.

You can access this tool in more than 20 languages, which makes it an excellent resource for those serving within multiethnic or cross-cultural situations. You can find more information about this resource here: https://www.cpp.com/products/mbti/index.aspx.

Enneagram

The enneagram is another paradigm for self-awareness that I have found useful. Unlike the MBTI®, many presentations of the enneagram tool have stronger spiritual overtones (though they're not necessarily tied to any particular faith). They also tend to have a more negative side, pointing out potential areas of fault, temptations, and inappropriate responses for each personality type. The enneagram describes nine different personality types (*ennea* is Greek for the number nine) and the detailed characteristics associated with each.

While this tool can be used to explore interpersonal dynamics, I have found it most useful for more deeply exploring who I am—increasing my awareness of my current foibles and helping me envision how I might grow with excellence. I believe it is more useful than the MBTI® as a guidebook for future growth and development, but less useful for exploring and appreciating present team dynamics.

That being said, I have had profitable conversations with my leaders about our differences using enneagram categories. As I've mentioned before, if you know your leader's weaknesses, you can more easily offer him or her valuable support, encouragement, and practical help. The enneagram provides a great platform for understanding yourself and those you work alongside.

Use of the enneagram tool does require a significant investment of time and energy. Much of the material is deep and may touch on sensitive issues. While the MBTI® provides fairly quick results and insights, the enneagram presents a significant journey just to figure out which of the nine types you are! I needed time for much reflection, re-reading, and conversation to derive the full benefit of this tool, but it has provided profound insight and helpful language for understanding myself.

Unlike the MBTI®, the enneagram is not owned by any particular organization or company, thus a wide variety of books and websites make use of this paradigm. I have found various works by Don Richard Riso, Russ Hudson, and Richard Rohr beneficial, and Jerome Wagner's *The Enneagram Spectrum of Personality Styles* provided the most approachable introduction to the paradigm.

FIRO®

Like the enneagram, the FIRO® (or FIRO-B®), the Fundamental Interpersonal Relations Orientation instrument, is another tool that enables a deeper internal examination. This tool presents three areas of interpersonal need—affection, control, and inclusion—and examines each along two dimensions: wanted (desiring others to initiate with you in a particular area) and expressed (your desire to initiate with others in an area). While focused on the individual, this tool is inherently relational; its scope is intended to help someone identify both desires and behaviors related to interacting with others.

The FIRO® tool can touch on sensitive emotional and psychological areas, often highlighting places of relational woundedness. However, sharing and discussing results with fellow team members can open up opportunities for communicating needs and expectations within the group. Those who take the FIRO® on their own and never explore the results with their team miss out on most of its value. The FIRO® is not as focused on personal growth (as the enneagram and KGI® are), but rather provides a valuable snapshot of your current state of interpersonal need, raising awareness and providing categories that you can use to express yourself to others. It is perhaps best used in a group context where there is already a foundation of trust and vulnerability. Complete details can be found here: https://www.cpp.com/products/firo-b/index.aspx.

> "The most competent followers know their weaknesses well"
> (*How to Be a Star*, 163).

Klein Group Instrument®

The Klein Group Instrument® for Effective Leadership and Participation in Teams (KGI®) is a unique tool that focuses on personal behavior within group contexts. It looks at skills and tendencies in four areas: leadership, negotiation orientation, task focus, and interpersonal focus. These are further divided into nine subscales, which include assertiveness, group facilitation, perspective taking, task implementation, and positive group affiliation.

I appreciate a number of characteristics about this tool. For one, it's based on responses to 59 straightforward questions and provides the flexibility for a user to either consider one's group involvement in general or in regard to a specific team. The tool is intended for groups that are intentionally working together for some specific goal or outcome, rather than being applicable to any gathering of people (such as for a social function).

Although some of the subscale definitions take a bit of work to differentiate, none of the language is too technical, and the tool is broad enough to be relevant to a wide variety of groups. Even though the KGI® is grounded in thorough research, the tool doesn't require the involvement of a formal consultant to administer and interpret your results (as the MBTI® and FIRO® do).

While the KGI® includes leadership as one of its major scales, it consistently speaks of leadership *functions* rather than a single leadership role and thus validates the ways that group members may contribute to these functions. It also affirms the value of growing as a group contributor without presupposing that everyone wants to or will become the group leader.

Although correlated to MBTI® results, the KGI® emphasizes behaviors more than personality traits. As a result, the basic report includes a number of observations and suggestions that users can develop as they seek to enhance their group participation. This direction toward generating a personal growth plan is far clearer than anything presented in the MBTI® or enneagram. At the same time, the KGI® takes a reasonable approach to personal development, recommending that users select only one item to invest in at a time, rather than trying to address all possible growth areas at once.

As you work on personal growth, the KGI® recommends involving others to provide input and feedback. A group option allows teams to compile individual team member profiles so the broader team's tendencies, strengths, and challenges can easily be identified. This dual emphasis on personal and group dynamics fits naturally within the perspective that excellent followership incorporates both individual growth and investment in relationships. Full information can be found here: http://www.capt.org/assessment-kgi/.

The Clarion Model

The Clarion Model also emphasizes both individual and group dynamics. I have found this resource so useful that every team I've been part of since 2006 has used it. Clarion's web-based framework of assessments and tools enables teams to understand and value members' differences and to work together effectively. It promotes efficiency in personal and team development by helping to surface relevant areas of growth and by providing vocabulary to use in conversations about those topics. Each member of an organization or team will be able to "self-revelate"—to present to others who they are, the distinctives of their personalities, preferences, values, and a summary of what they have to offer to the group (which Clarion refers to as your "best contributions"). I appreciate that the Clarion Model emphasizes the value of "personal development in the context of team development."

The Clarion model incorporates the MBTI®, FIRO®, and Lingenfelter's basic values model (see below) to draw insights, but it also has a number of internally developed assessments related to strengths/gifts, values, leadership styles, etc., to help construct a fairly well-rounded personal profile focused on answering the question, "Who am I?" From there, the model turns to helping your team answer similar questions, including "Who are we?" and "Where are we going?" and "What is my part?"[3]

An article from *The Economist* magazine[4] attributed the success of pop star Lady Gaga to the fact that she helps people address three of these same ideas. As the music and entertainment world has apparently discovered, it's valuable for all of us—in whatever organization, business, or association we may involve ourselves—to be able to respond to these fundamental questions.

There is currently only a Christian version of the Clarion Model available, though there's been some discussion about the development of a secular version as well. Clarion does require affiliation with an organization for the use of this tool (i.e., individuals cannot take themselves through the model). More information is available at www.clarionmodel.com.

Mentoring/Coaching

One of the most rewarding pursuits within personal development is to find a mentor or coach. While all of the tools we've listed are useful, nothing is more valuable than deep, ongoing conversation with people who can speak into your life and provide guidance and perspective. Whether you interact with people who are older, more knowledge-able, or more experienced than you (mentoring), or find someone who is willing to ask you the right questions to help you seek your own answers (coaching), the journey of personal development is best accomplished as a tandem pursuit.

> "Seek wise counsel" (*How to Be a Star at Work*, 169).

Getting others involved in your journey is critical. These others may be leaders or peers, from inside your organization or outside ... and, perhaps ideally, all of the above.[5] If you are going to take seriously the followership obligation of investing in your own personal development, I cannot emphasize more strongly the importance of involving others who are committed to accompanying you on that journey. A healthy community of support and encouragement is a truly valuable resource indeed.

Cross-Cultural Awareness

Current trends of global engagement have ensured that there are any number of resources and reference materials available to describe cross-cultural realities. I have previously mentioned the books *Cultural Intelligence: Living and Working Globally* by David Thomas and Kerr Inkson and *Cultures and Organizations: Intercultural Cooperation and Its Importance for Survival* by Geert Hofstede. Of the two, I recommend starting with *Cultural Intelligence*. It's an approachable book that lays out a good foundation for considering issues of cross-cultural relationship. Hofstede's work is useful, but rather technical. Some of David Livermore's books, including *Cultural Intelligence: Improving Your CQ to Engage Our Multicultural World*, serve as a specifically Christian resource in a similar vein to Thomas and Inkson's work.

Other helpful books include Sherwood Lingenfelter's *Ministering Cross-Culturally*. His basic values model presents six continuums of perspectives related to time, judgment, crises, goals, self-worth, and vulnerability. I have regularly made use of this paradigm in talking about differences that surface within a multicultural team dynamic. Perhaps the biggest critique of this book is that it is very American-centric in its references and comparisons. I understand that the book is currently under revision and look forward to seeing what improvements are made when it is re-released. Along the lines of Lingenfelter's work, James Plueddemann's *Leading Across Cultures* has also been commended to me as a useful resource.

I have also found useful *Cross-Cultural Servanthood* by Duane Elmer, which helps the reader shape a healthy perspective and response to engagement with other cultures, rather than imparting facts or paradigms for interactions. Founded on the premise of humility and approaching others in the posture of a learner, this book is of invaluable benefit to followership, closely aligning with the obligations and opportunities we have previously explored.

In our digital age, our smartphones may be more well-versed in cross-cultural information than we are. Various apps—such as "CultureCompass" by publisher itim International and "JPA iTraveler" by LGYtech—help navigate multicultural interactions. "CultureCompass" is an accessible presentation of

Hofstede's research that allows you to select two nations/regions from 50+ options and see a comparison of their scores on Hofstede's four dimensions of cultures. The app also provides a summary and brief exploration of what each dimension may look like. "JPA iTraveler" provides basic data about dozens of countries, but also includes helpful notes about various kinds of interactions, outlining behaviors that are appropriate and expected. Even though we ultimately relate to individual people and not to entire nations, having even this bit of background knowledge can help to construct a framework for speaking with someone of another culture, perhaps preventing a number of cultural *faux pas.*[6]

> "Diversity of cultural background is not just a problem to be solved; it is an opportunity to be capitalized on"
> (*Cultural Intelligence*, 131).

Finally, if you are willing to invest significant time and energy, availing yourself of language learning tools has incomparable value when seeking to bridge a cultural gap. Even if everyone involved in your group functions reasonably well in English, making the effort to foray into someone else's language provides you with insight into a new culture and perspective that may not come through in English. My own study of Mandarin Chinese, including a bit of Chinese character writing, provided significant insight into Chinese views of time and community. You will likely find that your efforts to understand and use a bit of someone's native language will yield huge dividends in your trust bank account. Your effort shows that you're committed to understanding that person, and it will therefore open additional doors for communication and understanding, which are the greatest resources of all.

12

CLARIFYING VISION AND ROLE

Self-awareness involves more than knowing your personality quirks or even your strengths and weaknesses. It requires deep questioning of what you want your life to be about and the goals and purposes you desire to achieve. From there, you have the additional task of envisioning a role that would enable you to pursue those aims. Many of us already have some sort of role; we don't come with a blank slate. Therefore, the task of gaining clarity within our current role—both about what we are responsible for and what we hope to achieve—can become even more difficult, but nonetheless essential.

Clarifying Vision

To offer the fullness of who we are to our organization, we must identify what we hope to accomplish through our involvement. Consider the following: What do you want the end results to be? How will you know if you have stewarded your time, energy, and skills with excellence? What personal passions are you hoping to tap into as a follower?

All too often, we followers may think that these self-directed questions are relatively unimportant. If we expect leaders to have all the vision and influence, to set pace and direction, we may unfortunately think it's not necessary to consider goal, mission, and purpose on our own.

On the other hand, we may already be asking ourselves a variety of questions—but perhaps not the most important ones. Robert Kelley advises that we must get beyond the simple question of "What kind of work do I want to do?" and move deeper, asking, "What do I want to achieve? What will I commit myself to?"[1] He also says that "purposeful commitment" is a key resource for followers; "The important point is to find something you care about."[2]

The pursuit of personal development—and the related tools mentioned in the previous chapter—can help you uncover your deeply rooted concerns, those causes you believe to be worth investing in. Knowing yourself is vital to fully understanding which endeavors you most desire to be a part of, as well as uncovering the possible challenges of that pursuit. For example, as I've learned more about my own unique abilities—which include a love for teaching—I have found clarity about what my contributions will look like within my organization. I've also been able to describe struggles that I face since I weigh my organization's core values to a different degree (or with a different priority) than many of my colleagues. This awareness has aided me in defining and differentiating my contribution, freeing me from the burden of comparing the nature of my role to the kind of work others are carrying out.

One key factor in defining your vision is motivation. What compels you to be involved or to seek a particular outcome?

> "Management of our life and health are even more fundamental than management of our work if we are to be reliable team members and a source of support for our leaders" (*The Courageous Follower*, 47).

That driving force will have a significant influence on the direction you will go. Geert Hofstede points out some cultural universals, as he references work done by David McClelland that identifies three basic types of motive: achievement, affiliation, and power.[3] These tend to combine with elements of Maslow's hierarchy of needs (specifically safety/security, belongingness, and esteem) to describe overarching motivational pairs such as achievement and esteem, or achievement and belongingness.[4] For instance, some people are motivated toward achievement because it gives rise to esteem and enhances their reputation and feelings of self-worth. Other people are motivated toward achievement because it leads to an enhancement of their group identity (belongingness), as a result of making a helpful contribution or participating in what the group is doing.

There are any number of motivators, both intrinsic and extrinsic, including recognition, responsibility, advancement, salary, organizational policies, and working conditions.[5] For some, the experience of working with a group will be even more important than the group's output. For others, stability may be the key motivator. In considering your vision, explore your motives. Achieving clarity here will guide you into finding an organization or role that will complement your internal drive, providing you with an environment in which you're able to grow and excel.

However, it's not enough to ask yourself vision-related questions. You must also be able to articulate your vision to others. The ability to relate to others your sense of passion, purpose, and desire is critical for being able to find roles that will be life-giving and satisfying, as well as a good fit in terms of your team's aims. As a follower, you do your leader (and yourself) a service by being able to communicate your motivations. "In order for a person to lead, he or she must be able to understand the basic motivation of those being led—their willingness to exert effort toward a goal."[6]

Books like *The Path: Creating Your Mission Statement for Work and for Life*, by Laurie Beth Jones, advocate for simple, brief mission statements that are so reflective of who you are and inherent to your being that you can rattle them off in an instant, even at gunpoint! However, you may prefer to capture more nuances about what you feel you're particularly wired to do and what outcomes you feel called to pursue. You may find it helpful to create a longer statement, even a narrative, to describe your aims.

My wife and I went through this process some years ago, during a significant season of transition. Faced with a number of opportunities, many of which seemed good, we struggled to figure out which one we were supposed to embrace. We ended up writing a vision statement for ourselves *as a couple*, recognizing that since we are bonded in matrimony, whatever the next season of life was to hold, we would be moving into it together. We spent time considering what abilities, gifts, passions, and interests we had as a couple, and then wrote out our summary. It ran to two paragraphs—hardly brief, and we couldn't recite it from memory—but it felt like an accurate depiction of who we are and what we wanted to be about in our next season of life.

The process of clarifying your vision/mission is a step forward in your personal development and self-awareness. But clarifying your vision also gives those whom you are—or hope to be—working with a better opportunity to understand you, to hear about your deep motivations and cares, and to help you in your role. Consider, craft, and communicate your vision, as you strive to follow well.

Clarifying Role

Having clarity about your role—whether it's a current one or one you're about to take on—will also contribute to your ability to follow well. A written-out role description can offer this kind of clarity. However, in my experience such descriptions exist mainly for levels of leadership—team leaders, managers, directors, coordinators. I have only rarely found a well-considered and clearly articulated set of expectations for conventional team members, participants, or volunteers. But whether they're captured in a concrete format or not, expectations do exist. The danger for us as followers, then, is that we may be held accountable for areas we're unaware of. Or, on the flipside, others may undervalue our roles, thinking that there are few areas that have been entrusted to us.

> "…You need to be clear minded about the organization's overall purpose, and you should make your decisions so your actions are clearly directed at that purpose. Your obligation is to build your own vision and to act strategically on behalf of your superior" (*Leading Up*, 220).

I mentioned in Chapter 4 that creating a description for *all* roles is a valuable step in establishing a healthy hierarchy, where all those involved—at any level and with any sphere of responsibility—feel validated and valued. While ultimately this task of clarifying roles belongs to our leaders—since we as followers usually don't get the final say on the matter—we can voice our need for clarity and talk with others about how to achieve it.

I recently consulted for a team working in Eastern Europe. Although the leadership positions had been filled by the same people for 10 years, one member finally voiced that she was feeling a disconcerting lack of clarity about what her role actually was. She had long lived in limbo about what was expected of her, what she was empowered to do, and how her role interfaced with the other team members. A decade of ambiguity! Clearly, this is not the kind of environment that promotes a healthy team or excellent followership.

Thankfully, she didn't give up and resign herself to a place of uncertainty. Instead, she worked with the team leader and then brought in outside help to address this inhibiting lack of role definition. From a place of discouragement, and even disengagement, she has now moved into a place of thriving contribution. To do so, she worked on personal development and identified her strengths, then worked with others to assess the team's needs and concretely articulate her responsibilities within that dynamic.

Some situations warrant the creation of highly nuanced and individualized role descriptions—one for each member of the organization. Oftentimes, however, a sound starting place is simply to craft general documents that relate to those in leadership and those who serve as the majority of an endeavor—followers. Avoid fixating on establishing titles or creating stratification within the organization; "outline responsibility, not rank."[7] The goal should be to designate who is doing what so that each member understands and values the contribution of everyone else.

A group who undertakes this process will likely be able to uncover where vital areas are being overlooked and unassigned—tasks where everyone says, "I thought it was so-and-so's responsibility to do that." This process also helps to identify where certain items have been delegated to someone for whom they will be a rather poor fit. (The Clarion Model tool mentioned previously has a number of resources that speak to this very issue.)

One approach for creating position descriptions is to begin with your leader's job description. Those in leadership positions often have an existing list of responsibilities. Beginning there, draft your own document by exploring which expectations also apply to you, as a subordinate of this particular leader, and brainstorm what additional tasks you should be taking on so that your leader can best accomplish what's been delegated to him or her.

Other avenues for considering your contribution include returning to the larger purpose of your organization or team and bringing in your personal vision statement to creatively explore what you have to offer the group. Turn your areas of strength, ability, and passion into a well-defined aspect of your followership. Then you'll be able to fulfill your obligations and pursue opportunities that will be both satisfying to you and beneficial for your team.

Clarifying your role is a two-part process. There is one aspect embedded in the organization—the big picture, the requirements and expectations laid upon you. But there is a second aspect that originates within you, with identifying and articulating what you bring to the table, what various skills and vision you steward within your sphere of involvement. You can best serve yourself and your organization by considering both, and thus taking a step forward in following with excellence.

13

REST AS A RESOURCE

The Red Zone

A few years ago, I helped shape a leadership development initiative. Part of the required reading for the program included a single chapter from the book *Growing Leaders* by James Lawrence. In Chapter 4 of the book, titled "Living in the Red Zone," Lawrence uses the analogy of a car's tachometer—the gauge that registers how fast the engine is spinning (in RPMs, revolutions per minute)—a measure of how hard it is working. All tachometers have a portion marked in red; at a certain level of RPMs, the engine works dangerously hard, and continuing at this level of output will eventually lead to overheating or engine failure.

Lawrence uses this model to call attention to our modern proclivity to running ourselves beyond a safe level of output. We all have a certain capacity level, and we may be able to work a bit beyond that for a season, but to remain at that heightened level of engagement will lead to burnout and fatigue. We need times to relax, to come back down to normal levels, to recuperate, to alleviate the output stress we place on ourselves—or we risk long-term ineffectiveness or crashing. Lawrence also high-lights five areas of our lives where warning lights may indicate that we're living in the red zone: physical, emotional, relational, intellectual, and spiritual.

As I look around, I can easily spot leaders who live perpetu-ally in the red zone. With their broad scope of responsibilities, multiple constituencies, and array of subordinates, it's not surprising that many leaders regularly work at a level of output that exceeds their healthy level of capacity. It is sometimes harder for us to evaluate ourselves as followers and to consid-er whether we, too, have adopted a similar pattern, working ourselves into physical, emotional, relational, intellectual, or spiritual unhealth.

Part of the difficulty in avoiding the red zone is that it can be highly productive. A car revved up to many thousands of RPMs is flying down the road, eating up the miles in no time. Productivity at this level is often obvious—and satisfying. With such output, we may find it difficult to question whether we *should* be continuing in this way. Questions of how long we can keep this up are often buried beneath our glowing performance evaluations and acclaim from our leaders.

There is a significant lesson here for us. When we consider capacity, our tendency is to try and determine what we *can* do: What are the abilities, talents, and other resources that I can contribute to my group's project? But there is a more important issue that lies at the heart of our red zone battle. Our capacity is not determined by what we *can* do, but by what we *should* do.

> "An intentional and community-based schedule of rest can be invaluable"
> (*I Am a Follower*, 127).

Just as each car has an indi-vidually calibrated red zone level, so too each of us has a personal level of healthy capacity. Tasks or situations or relationships take up a varying portion of our capac-ity, and that may be less or more than their effect on someone else.

Our goal is to establish a healthy pattern of engagement by understanding our particular capacity and how various realms of life, work, and responsibility draw upon our finite amount of physical, emotional, relational, intellectual, and spiritual resources.

From there, we can establish a healthy level of continuous output by saying yes and no at the right times to the opportunities that come our way. Just because I have a spare 30 minutes in my day does not mean that I should (or must) fill it with whatever comes along. Those 30 minutes may be the brief period of slowdown that my engine (life) needs to recuperate to continue in effective output. Maybe a better or more fitting opportunity will come along later—one for which I wouldn't have time or energy if I immediately say yes to whatever is currently in front of me.

On the other hand, red zone caution shouldn't serve as an excuse for laziness; 30 minutes of unallocated time doesn't necessarily mean that I should stare into space and do nothing. Being a good steward of that time may mean a variety of things. Should I go looking for another project? Or should I say yes to whatever comes along? Perhaps engage in some maintenance or administrative tasks? Are there other life-giving investments that will be productive, both for my organization and my own state of health, energy, and satisfaction?

The decision to say yes or no becomes a difficult dilemma when the opportunity in front of me is a good one—something that I can do, something that is needed, something I may enjoy ... or all of the above. A sense of self-awareness, built within a communal process of personal development and accompanied by clarity in your personal vision, can provide helpful rubrics for rightly knowing when to say yes or no. Along with Lawrence, I acknowledge the wisdom of Stephen Covey in saying, "The greatest incentive to say *no* is to have an even greater *yes* burning inside you."[1]

Rest

However successful we may be in identifying our true capacity and assessing our current level of output, the antidote to our plague of busyness and burnout is not merely developing more efficient procedures and improving our abilities. Instead, we must arm ourselves with a new tactic in the battle for healthy productivity: rest.

My thinking about rest has developed significantly in the past eight years. Issues of boundaries, rhythm (what some would call "Sabbath"), and vacation have significantly shaped my own followership.

For a good portion of my life, I've worked from home. While such a situation has a number of benefits, it comes with the challenge of never truly being able to leave work "at the office," at a geographically distant location that would preclude me from writing, editing, and checking email each time I walk past my home computer. Of course, with the prevalence of laptops and smartphones, those working in a traditional office environment still face many of the same temptations during off-hours. Boundaries are vital for all of us.

My own situation is further complicated in that my wife and I both work for the same organization, and we both work primarily from home. We thus both face the continual siren call to check email *just one more time*. Within this framework, I discovered a significant truth: If I choose to give into that siren call, I may force my wife to do the same.

Although we have separate roles within our organization, we work together on a number of projects. So consider: I check my email. I get asked a quick question requiring a brief answer, but one that I don't have. My wife, however, would know the answer. So then I end up asking her a work question. She may not know the answer offhand, so she may sit down at her computer to find the necessary information. While there, she checks her own email, a new round of inquiries comes in, and off we go ...

almost like we never left the office. She isn't free to rest because I did not keep a healthy boundary.

The profound truth is that my decisions to work or to rest have a direct affect on others. By deciding to work, I effectively force my teammate/coworker/wife to work as well.

Within the Jewish and Christian faiths, this observation is formalized by a commandment from God. As part of the Ten Commandments, God requires that his people should regularly rest, ceasing from work every seventh day. This commandment refers to keeping the Sabbath (which means "to stop or cease"), and God provides crucial insight when he gives this mandate to Moses. In Deuteronomy 5:14, one of the foundations for this order is *so that* those who work for you can also rest. If a landowner chooses to work, he forces his hired laborers to be out in the field with him. And in my case, if a husband can't resist checking his work email from home, he drags his wife along with him.

Although many leaders seek to model diligence and hard work for their followers, we are tied to one another in this work-rest dynamic. A leader may intend to sacrifice only himself or herself, working extra hours to help keep the group on track. While the desire may be to alleviate the burdens of others, such a habit can actually serve to steal the opportunity for subordinates to rest. Equally, my choice as a follower to work "out of bounds" to get ahead with my tasks may unintentionally apply pressure on my leader to continue to engage in his or her work (often by responding to my emails) beyond a healthy boundary.

> "Keeping a balanced life is the best thing that you can do for yourself and your leader" (Armstrong, *Followership*, 120).

By intentionally stopping—whether each evening, each weekend, or according to another established pattern—we have the opportunity to keep a proper perspective on our capacity and involvement. As followers, we must strike a balance between extremes: between valuing our contribution, and believing the weight of the world rests on our shoulders alone. When we see that the world doesn't crumble without our active engagement for a time, we can draw back from the pressure and anxiety we may feel to perform at red-zone levels. We may be able to more fully appreciate the value of our team and coworkers, seeing how they can carry on without us or, better yet, how we can all stop together to rest and celebrate what we have accomplished.

For our rest to be helpful, it must come from a place of good stewardship. It is possible for rest to be unhealthy; we usually call this laziness. For a break to be the relaxing, refreshing blessing it is intended to be, it should follow a time of diligent work.[2] After a time of performing quality labor, a time of rest can indeed be a celebration of what has been accomplished, a satisfying reflection that—for today, for this week, for this term—I have done well and I have done enough. Perhaps I *could* have done more, but I can be content with fulfilling my "shoulds" for this time.

This leads me to a final thread of thought about rest. Boundaries are important, directly tied to our choice to rest and the ability of others to rest as well. But an additional resource for following well is to have a right perspective on the interplay between work and rest. There is a bit of a chicken-and-egg story here that we do not reflect on often enough.

It's common in a Western, North American context, for us to take the perspective that we work *in order to* rest. We work hard because we want to play hard. We go to the office every day so that we can accrue vacation time and eventually get a bit of down time to do what we want to do. We labor and then we earn the reward of a two-week holiday.

A dear friend of mine shared a contrasting perspective with me: He encouraged me to take the approach that, rather than working to rest, I should rest *in order to* work. Rather than conceiving of down time as an opportunity to bring my red-zone counter back into safe parameters or to replenish all my spent personal resources, I can take a proactive view of seeing my rest time as preparation for work. Rather than being the result or reward of work, rest can be the readying for work.[3]

Perhaps you—like me and many of my friends—have had this experience: You're finally able to take your weeklong vacation and on the very first day, you become ill. Your body just seems to collapse into sickness now that you've let up a bit from your regularly strenuous pace. By the end of the week, your sickness may have passed, but you hardly feel ready to get back into things. You're still exhausted and already beginning to count the days until the next long weekend or bit of holiday when you might try again for that needed rest.

Now imagine a different scenario: You have worked well, saying yes and no as your capacity requires and your clarified role description allows. It is now time to stop. You have a chance to change your pace and routine significantly, to take a deeply satisfied breath and to prepare yourself—physically, emotionally, relationally, mentally, and spiritually—for another period of work.

Rather than loathing the return to the office, you can rest to ready yourself for another round of helpful service and contribution: diligently stewarding, faithfully submitting, authentically honoring, and fully participating. And this does not just have to be a once- or twice-yearly opportunity; nurturing this perspective can be a part of your weekly, and even daily, times of stopping.

The only way I was able to create that healthy rhythm was to learn to live with good boundaries. I now daily discipline myself to stop work. I give myself regular opportunities for doing non-work things. I explore life-giving creative outlets. I enjoy my marriage and spend time with friends. Now the larger periods of rest—whether weekends or weeks—have taken on the flavors of a backward-looking celebration and a forward-looking preparation.

As human beings, we are far more than mere production machines,[4] and our down times should be far richer than opportunities for bare-bones maintenance. We should experience delight in doing what we were made to do—which requires self-awareness and clarity of vision—and we should live from a place of proactive preparation rather than reactive desperation.

Vacations and holidays for my wife and me have become times to embrace unique opportunities rather than recover from burnout. But making this transformation has required mutual commitment to boundaries; concern and respect for how our choices affect one another; and regular habits of celebration, thankfulness, and planning.

Part 4

FOLLOWERSHIP IN RELATIONSHIP WITH LEADERS

As I've mentioned more than once now, being intentional in your relationship with your leader is a critical factor in excellent followership. The nature of your relationship with your leader will significantly shape your followership journey, from counteracting misconceptions to opening up ways for you to contribute. An acquaintanceship characterized by hostility, antagonism, and manipulation will result in a very different platform for your involvement than an open partnership founded on trust, cooperation, and a commitment to understanding and forgiveness. Where and how you direct your energies, your degree of satisfaction, and your effectiveness are all affected by your working dynamic with your leader.

14

THE LEADER-FOLLOWER DYNAMIC

Followership is inherently relational; at the very minimum, your status as a follower implies some degree of connection to someone who is in a position of oversight, authority, or responsibility. The flavor of your particular followership is essentially defined by your responses to the person in that leadership role.[1] However, many of us followers can likely agree with this observation by Robert Kelley: "The most important but troublesome relationship for many followers is with the leader."[2] We cannot presume that we will automatically have easy, mutually affirming, productive relationships with our superiors.

Instead, you should anticipate that your connection with your leader will require a significant investment of time, energy, awareness, and intentionality if it is to enable—not hinder—your ability to follow well. Commit to "being superior at being subordinate."[3] While some of that pursuit is internal—as part of your journey of personal development—a significant portion stems from developing your relationship with your leader.

When something goes wrong in an organization, most people try to assign blame. Was this result a failure of leadership, or was it the outcome of incompetent followership? Was there a lack of vision, or was there insubordination that led to the lack of achievement? I regularly come across articles online that seek to determine whether current situations in Nigeria are a fault of leadership or followership. Both sides have representation, and some authors even venture to posit that both sides share blame. But few, if any, have dared to explore a different question: Whether the lack of effectiveness—in a government, business, association, or club—is fundamentally a result of the quality of the *relationship* between the leader and followers.

> "Many if not most of [the changes that are occurring in organizations] involve a fundamental rethinking and renegotiation of the way people at all levels manage their relationship with people in authority" (*It Takes Two*, xi).

In his book *It Takes Two*—an exploration of the interaction between superiors and subordinates— Gene Boccialetti considers a few overt examples of failure involving catastrophes such as shipping collisions and plane crashes. He concludes, "The tragedy ... is thus more than a failure of leadership and also more than a failure of followers. It is better understood as a failure of the boss-subordinate *relationship*."[4] Our downfalls may be more complex than laying blame on one side or the other. We're more prone to "systems failure" or "relationship failure" than we usually identify.[5] It is for this reason that we must consider our working relationships with our leaders as major components of our followership.

However, I'm not saying you should forsake the pursuit of effectiveness and productivity to focus solely on a pleasing friendship.[6] Instead, acknowledge that your connection to your leader is a result of some purpose; you and your leader are working toward a communal goal within your organization. Still, within that framework, you can strive to have a true relationship with your leader, "a relationship in which [you] can comfortably meet a leader as one human being to another."[7]

Much of our ability to overcome our own misconceptions about followership relies on viewing our leaders as people with needs very similar to our own. Likewise, our bosses must be able to see us as real people with legitimate needs, perspectives, and resources to offer. But "getting along well"—and we all have differing definitions of what this would mean—"while important, should not be your highest aspiration."[8] Rather, explore what sort of relationship would be most appropriate for your working dynamic, that is, the kind of interaction that leads to individuals thriving *and* furthering the organization's goals. As you do so, avoid relegating relationship to a mere corporate strategy or best practice guideline.

Different kinds of work require different follower-leader dynamics. "Innovative tasks require certain kinds of interaction that are different from routine tasks, developmental tasks, or crisis situations."[9] In some cases, creative tension and differing perspectives lead to higher quality results. In other situations, harmony and agreement will lead to group accomplishment.

Both your and your boss' expectations for the working relationship will factor into the nature of your cooperative dynamic. Desires for influence and appropriate workplace intimacy may differ significantly, and holding too tightly to the desire for "getting along well" may only lead to mutual frustration and ultimate ineffectiveness.

Given that we are discussing the complex interplay between people, there is no end to the degree of variety that can exist within a leader-follower relationship. That being said, in the next few chapters we'll explore some of the most essential and universal elements of the follower-leader dynamic.

15

COMMUNICATION AND TRUST

Like all relationships, the one between leaders and followers rests on two fundamental qualities: communication and trust. Healthy and effective relationship requires both dialogue and a belief in the authenticity of the other person's words and actions. I've worked with many teams who have established an expectation that communication should be "HOT"—honest, open, and transparent. This type of communication creates a platform from which to navigate all other relational and workplace challenges. Although culture influences such workplace norms, without some communication and trust resource—and it is indeed a resource, requiring investment, refinement, judicious use, and stewardship—almost nothing else can be accomplished.

A great deal has already been written about trust and communication in relationship—a lot of which I wholeheartedly agree with. I'm switching up the format below to invite others into the dialogue. In bold are quotations from others I've found particularly insightful, followed by my own reflection.

"Communication between leaders and followers must be upwards and downwards."[1] Dialogue is key. We cannot, must not, content ourselves with merely receiving memos from on high. Even if we feel comfortable receiving a large amount of direction from our superiors, it's essential that we send communication back up the chain. Our leaders need the information and perspectives we can offer. Of course, sharing this information may present challenges: "Information is more than words: it is words which fit into a cultural framework."[2] We must be sure to communicate in such a way that the information we want to share can actually be received and understood. Some leaders may not be very open to receiving input, but this reality only further necessitates our efforts to cultivate a trusting relationship, thus bridging this gap as much as possible. If we have a history of integrity and reliability, that track record will establish a conduit we can use to serve even our resistant leaders.

"Without leaders and followers responding reciprocally with each other in positive ways, leadership never occurs, community ... is never established, and the organization flounders."[3] Communication on its own is not enough. Poor communication won't lead to an improved relationship—unless we work through that miscommunication in a healthy way. We must be intent on *responding positively* to one another. This requires us to listen to one another and endeavor to hear the intended message rather than presuming we understand correctly. Responding positively means that we resist the urge to lash out with a hollow retort—such as name-calling, false accusations, or blame—and instead commit to sharing and clarifying our own perspective and feelings.

"Followers must be willing to allow the leader(s) to misunderstand them and receive the likely negative emotional response from the leaders at such a challenge."[4] We cannot expect that our words will always be well received, especially if they question or critique a leader's decision. Communicating involves an element of risk. There's always potential for misunderstandings and defensiveness. This is why creating a foundation of trust is so vital. We must continually maintain and add to that foundation so that, when the time comes, a bit of upheaval will not bring the whole building down. Another analogy refers to making regular trust deposits into your joint account at Fidelity Bank. That way, when the need arises, you can make a withdrawal and the mutual relationship will still have a balance to fall back on.

"Do not try to play a role unless you can be genuinely enthusiastic about it. It might cost a huge price if you cast yourself in a role that you do not believe you can fill."[5] In our desire to follow well, we may sometimes allow our eagerness to outstrip our honesty. In an effort to relieve our leaders' burdens— or to take on a new opportunity—we may be tempted to offer that which we don't have to contribute. When we communicate, we must do so honestly if we are to build up the trust account. If we cannot personally fill a gap in an organization, or if we cannot actually help by removing tasks from our leaders' plates, then we should express our care, concern, and awareness, but stop short of making promises and offers that we cannot fulfill. Doing so will only lead to disappointment and ineffectiveness, and may actually multiply the burden we were seeking to ease. In the long term, our trust account will take a severe hit, and it will require a substantial investment to rebuild it and return to a position where we're able to offer real assistance in the future. We don't want to contribute evidence to this observation: "As a leader, the hardest to deal with is an unfaithful servant."[6]

"Relationships are not the result of strategic maneuvering; they are born and grow through genuine concern for others and through cumulative experience."[7] Associating the idea of relationship so closely with the workplace can make it seem that interaction with your leader is simply one more task, or one more challenge to overcome. The dynamic between you and your superior can begin to take on the air of a simple means to an end. We must remember that our aim is to relate to another human being—not to manipulate a system or to grease the cogs of the machinations of the powers that be. We are engaging with another person. Ironically, to reduce our relationship to a strategic outcome or corporate asset is to dehumanize the bond.

At times, we may need to ask ourselves, "Am I engaging this way out of genuine concern for my leader, or am I merely executing a plan for personal and corporate effectiveness?" One way to maintain the human element is by valuing and engaging in "cumulative experience"—opportunities that require working closely together, coupled with refreshing times of celebration, fun, and play. This pursuit of common experience is another valuable aspect of communication and trust-building that is all too easy to minimize since its value only shows up in the long-term and its effect on the bottom line is less obvious.

"Not only must we tell leaders *how* we feel, but we must tell them how *intensely* we feel about the issues that concern us."[8] I have recently been on a journey (fueled in part by my use of the enneagram) of becoming more aware of my own internal expectations, and how they relate to working within a team. For example, I'm learning that I need to communicate my feelings and expectations to my teammates. That way, rather than responding in anger or frustration after the fact, I can clue them into my feelings ahead of time or at the outset of a particular endeavor. To do this, I must be disciplined in self-awareness and come to grips with what I see as important and to what extent. I value a lot of things, but I can let go of some of them. However, when other things I value are overlooked or ignored, I respond much stronger and it feels much more personal. But regardless of whether things can or will happen "my way," my obligation to create healthy relationship means I must relate these things to my leader (and perhaps the whole team) in a way that accurately reflects their significance to me. Doing so builds trust as we create a group experience where we talk through individual team members' feelings on a particular issue. We may be at fault for our own unmet needs because we fail to speak up. "Even a well-intentioned and genuinely interested boss would find it difficult to know how to assist you, sponsor you, or channel resources to support you unless you make your attitudes quite clear."[9]

"Work can become very stressful and lonely if you maintain high distance [relational separation] everywhere. Find someone to talk to. If one of those people is not your boss, you are in big trouble."[10] If you cannot talk to your leader, you run the risk of putting yourself in a place where you have issues, needs, or ideas but no one who is able to help you. The position of leader is usually unique in its stewardship of resources, influence, and authority. If you're unable to communicate with your leader, you will almost ensure your exclusion from access to these organizational assets. The danger with having communicative relationships with only your peer followers is that it is far too tempting to fall into grumbling, complaining, and gossiping about the leader or situation. Humanizing and actively talking with your leader helps to combat these negative habits and at the same time opens the door to getting the support and assistance you may need.

16

COOPERATION AND PRE-FORGIVENESS

Our leader-follower relationships also require cooperation: individuals working together to achieve a single aim. Even if one person plays the role of devil's advocate, seemingly in opposition to the leader or other team members, such a role done well—not merely for the sake of argument—ultimately works toward achieving the community's purpose. Without this common purpose, cooperation is impossible: It is the hub around which we focus our mutual participation in fulfilling a shared vision, especially since our specific tasks may be very different.

Cooperation involves more than simply agreeing on an overarching aim. For the sake of relationship, we must also agree with how to go about achieving this outcome. If we fail at this level of agreement, we still miss out on a cooperative relationship, since our efforts to accomplish our common purpose will be surrounded by conflict. Gene Boccialetti goes so far as to say, "If people do not understand and accept where they are heading, *and* how they are supposed to get there, they cannot function even semiautonomously."[1] If we operate primarily on our own, we will face extreme difficulty in completing our tasks because we neglect the cooperation that will help us achieve our purpose.

Tensions, criticism, and conflict—from us toward others, or from others toward us—surrounding our work will hamper us from effectively moving forward to achieve our goal. We'll waste time and energy on defending our course of action. While highlighting different perspectives and approaches may ultimately lead to greater effectiveness, the relationship will have no synergy if it perpetually exists in this state of disagreement and incongruence. Fundamentally, a cooperative relationship requires a consensus about both where we are going and how we will get there.

"Followers and leaders work together better when they are comfortable with each other, and value congruence is one way to achieve common ground."[2] The unfortunate relational reality, however, is that even if we may agree on both purpose and methods, we may still struggle to work *with* our leaders to achieve our shared goals. What may seem like an ideal foundation for a cooperative relationship may instead become a platform to engage in an adversarial relationship with our bosses. If we wish "to be like the boss, to surpass the boss, to defeat the boss, or to resist the boss,"[3] we'll have a hard time working together. All of these leader-follower dynamics may exist within a certain level of values congruence. But while being like the boss or surpassing the boss may contribute to some degree of cooperation, striving to defeat or resist the boss are not likely to contribute to the effectiveness of your group.

> "The antidote to resentment is gratitude: the conviction that, despite our disappointments, others have contributed to our lives, and we are the better for it"
>
> (*Reworking Authority*, 100).

Sometimes, these aggressive perspectives arise from a sense of dissatisfaction with the leader's performance. If I place a high value on the organization's purpose or I believe strongly in the methods being used to reach that purpose, I may become frustrated at the shortcomings of my leader. In such a case, I may perceive my leader as an inhibitor to fulfilling the goal, and thus it may be tempting for me to overcome such a boss in an attempt to remove the obstacle as I see it.

While our foundation of communication and trust should allow us to address a leader's mistakes, we must also intentionally develop habits of forgiveness and *pre*-forgiveness as other essential aspects of the follower-leader relationship.

Let's pause and remember again that leaders are people too. They aren't superhuman, infallible, or almighty. By holding such a view, we (ironically) constrain our leaders and confine them to behavioral boundaries which we approve of. When they wander out of bounds, we launch into judgment and criticism. Perhaps we have some positive motive here, wanting to help our leaders keep to the straight and narrow, but all too often we fail to acknowledge that we don't hold ourselves to the same standards we apply to our leaders. We expect from them what we ourselves could never hope to deliver, and then elevate ourselves to the position of judge when errors or failings inevitably arise.

True enough, a healthy relationship will likely include a certain degree of mutual accountability; the foundation of open communication and trust should enable us to point out or ask about perceived inconsistencies. Likewise, our leader will usually have authority and responsibility to check up on us. So while our efforts to guard our leader from waywardness may be legitimate, the only way we can fulfill this responsibility is to establish an attitude of pre-forgiveness.

This aspect of relationship is one-sided, an internal view we carry with us—daily—into our interactions with our superiors and with our peers. It stems from the truth that we cannot expect perfection in ourselves, and so we cannot expect it from others either. Rather, learn to anticipate failures, disappointments, frustrations, mistakes, errors, and misjudgments in the words and actions of your leader. But instead of anticipating such things in a pessimistic way, default to an attitude of forgiveness. Don't allow yourself to be caught off guard if your unrealistic view of your leader becomes shattered when he or she makes a mistake. Avoid being knocked off balance relationally and emotionally when something goes awry, and don't retaliate with harsh words of judgment and criticism. Instead, commit to pre-forgiveness, which will enable you to still work with your leader in the midst of his or her failing—rather than abandoning or opposing him or her—and to do so from a pre-established foundation of healthy relationship, with their dignity and humanity in mind.

Too often we seem to apply a zero tolerance policy. Certainly, there can be egregious errors that warrant legal accusations or dismissal, and some mistakes will bring about consequences or the need for restitution. But is an error of judgment that results in profit loss or a mistaken decision that leads to missed deadlines rightfully within this category? I have regularly read of government officials and business leaders in certain countries who are honor-bound to commit suicide in the wake of their failing. What a tragedy! In such cases, the organization loses an otherwise valuable human resource, often because of a single misstep. You might recall my earlier comments about overdrawing one's trust account at Fidelity Bank; many constituencies are happy to close the account as soon as a single withdrawal is made. It is our role as followers to extend forgiveness and understanding where appropriate and to resist the tendencies of groupthink and mob mentality that lead us to vilify someone who is just as human as we are.

As with any toddler who stumbles before walking reliably, we should expect that our growing leaders will similarly need encouragement and approval rather than dismissal. In the short-term, we may struggle to express patience and tolerance when our leaders' errors in judgment seem commonplace. In our role as faithful followers, however, we should extend forgiveness and understanding. Relying on the relationship I have with my leader will help me to look past superficial mistakes and to see his or her heart, desire, and journey. We must remember that a growing leader has the ultimate goal of becoming the best version of who she or he truly is and contributing to the community in a yet more excellent way.

This attitude of pre-forgiveness can also enhance our relationship with our leader by reminding us of our involvement and the necessity for humility. A leader's failings are not solely his or her responsibility; others may be culpable as well. What if we had labored more faithfully, supplied better information, done our own due diligence? Would our leader have been able to make the right decision? If we contributed all that we had to the effort, would the leader's risky venture have succeeded? Pre-forgiveness can help us keep in mind that our community dynamic consists of many interrelationships; we are all strands in the same spiderweb, to use our earlier analogy. Perhaps if we and our peers had drawn tighter together around our leader, the gap in the web might not have been so destructive. Before we lay judgment or condemnation on our leader, we should spend some worthwhile time considering how much of the responsibility for a given shortcoming rests on our own shoulders.

> "Often people who are serving leaders don't understand that their leaders are going to be changing and developing right in front of their eyes"
> (Armstrong, *Followership*, 152).

17

INFLUENCE, SUBMISSION, AND REWARD

Influence can be a one-way street, in either direction: top-down or bottom-up. Each of us behind the wheel of a car experiences top-down influence: The traffic light decrees when we may move. No amount of honking or banging the wheel makes any difference; the light has its way. On the other hand, consider the early days of an infant's life. Undoubtedly, the parents are the authority figures, but in nearly every aspect of life, the influence flows from the child to the parents. No amount of reasoning or attempts at discipline can compete with the wailings of a newborn in need. The child's desires determine the family's schedule; even the parents' choice to sleep falls into the grip of this influential infant.

While many of us encounter both of these situations in life, neither are environments we would choose to remain in. The child must grow and develop and become a participating member of family life. Even the tyranny of the traffic light can be replaced by two-way influence. My time in the U.K. has shown me the possibilities for roadway give-and-take in traffic circles (roundabouts) and narrow streets that often require an interaction between jousting drivers. By getting into the driver's seat, you are expressing an expectation that others will yield to you and that you will yield to others, depending on what the circumstances and the law require.

I suggest that you also view your relationship with your leader as an avenue for two-way influence. Avoid coming into an organization as some do, "who are, for whatever reasons, simply resistant to any form of external guidance. They tend to see any direction and structure from the boss as an unwarranted intrusion on their professional or personal autonomy."[1] Affiliating yourself with an office, business, committee, or association requires some degree of setting aside personal autonomy—if your membership and involvement is going to offer any real substance. Regard your leader as "part of the team,"[2] a true coworker, a fellow part of the network of which you, too, are vital. Learn to expect and even hope that your leader's life will shape your own, and make a similar offer to put your unique human resources at the service of your leader.

The modern notion of "participatory servant leadership," which is en vogue in many organizations, provides a helpful paradigm for considering this kind of two-way influence. Leaders must do "leaderly" things like make difficult decisions and exercise judgment. At the same time, they must serve in the trenches, seemingly disrobed of their splendor as a superior and prepared to receive direction and input from others. As followers, then, we must faithfully fulfill our subordinate role while not shying away from exerting appropriate influence on those who hold responsibility and stewardship over us. If we are able to both respectfully give influence and receive influence, then we are on our way to establishing an effective relationship dynamic—one that allows all those involved to give their best contributions, without being constrained by titles.

Jimmy Collins, in his book *Creative Followership*, says, "Rather than looking for a job, look for a boss."[3] This concept is central to Collins' formulation for following well. Choose someone under whom you will have an opportunity to experience and exert influence. From this initial choice, you can derive significant staying power for the road ahead: "Remind yourself ... why you do what you do—you have chosen a boss to stand behind and support."[4] This perspective can help bolster your commitment to submit, which is always a necessary guardrail for exercising influence. For example, even if I have a superior who is receptive to input, my opportunity for influence does not guarantee that things will go my way. My leader may ultimately make a choice that is at odds with my feelings or opinion. If I am in an unhealthy working relationship, I may turn away in disgust, frustration, or hopelessness, believing that it is futile to try to influence upward since my opinions apparently have no real impact. Or I may dismiss my leader as inept, unwise, autocratic, or stupid to ignore my words. But realizing that I have chosen a relationship with this authority figure should bring me to a place of appropriate submission; it is my obligation as a follower and the proper response within my leader-follower relationship.

If we as followers are to achieve the attitude and action of submission, we'll need to invest significant effort in personal growth and internal discipline. The human nature in all of us inclines toward rebellion and having our own way, so we will need to cultivate a perspective of submission within our followership relationship. We need to own the reality that "particularly careful self-management by the subordinate is called for or the relationship can become quite stressed and tattered."[5] If we remain unbending, insisting on our own way, we can destroy whatever foundation of trust, communication, and values alignment we may have built through previous investment. We can condemn our relationship with our leader by failing to tame our resistance to submission. This underscores for us the necessity of an ongoing personal journey of development.

It's worth asking ourselves a few questions as we go on. First, how do we respond to someone else being in a position of responsibility and oversight above us? Gene Boccialetti proposes that we may be energetic, conscientious, or passive.[6] Do we engage cooperatively and wholeheartedly? Do we do more than our duty, or do we simply try to keep from hindering the leader's direction? On the negative side of things, are we overtly antagonistic? Do we engage in passive-aggressive behavior? Our general attitudes toward leadership and involvement will shine through in our specific interactions.

> "A follower's potential for influencing a leader will depend on the quality of relationship that has been developed between them" (*The Courageous Follower*, 81).

Let's consider the quality of our influence. In our interaction with our leaders, are we seeking influence for the benefit of the organization, or are we currying favor? Is our involvement and interaction with our leader focused on our own well-being within the organization, or are we honestly trying to contribute to the fulfillment of the group's aims? One author compares the former approach to manipulation or whining.[7] Remember that infantile influence is one-way influence, and it deprives us, our leader, and our organization of the fullness of our relationship-based synergy and cooperation.

As followers, we will often factor the notion of reward into our involvement in a particular endeavor. Whether we anticipate a reward of salary, significance, affiliation, legacy, or some other accolade, there is usually an explicit expectation of exchange—a transactional nature to our involvement. We give of ourselves, and we get something in return.

It's significant for us to remember that, like influence, this reward power shouldn't be one-way either. Rusty Ricketson reminds us that "followers also have reward power in rewarding their leaders with their following."[8] This journey of pursuing excellence in our followership equips us, in part, to provide this kind of reward: to be a valuable co-laborer to our leader and organization by making the most of our follower role. More specifically, even though we may not be *obligated* to do so, we should maintain an awareness of the *valuable opportunity* we have to reward our leader through affirmation and encouragement. Making a regular habit of bestowing this kind of reward on our leaders (and our peers as well) adds another layer to the significance of our relationships.

In addition to empowering our leaders by affirming their stewardship, in giving rewards we also contribute to creating a foundation of open communication and trust. A deeper, more personal connection can result from authentically offering words, acts of service, and even gifts. Such activities on our part can solidify our account status at the Fidelity Bank—perhaps not as a substantial deposit, but as a balance check that keeps us in good standing as credible depositors.

As with influence, here again we must search our motives. Are we offering reward solely to curry favor and to secure our own well-being? First and foremost, we must offer these rewards for the encouragement and well-being of our leader, and not for the purpose of manipulating the environment to our present or future advantage. Our rewards must be offered genuinely, without being contingent on the leader's future response in kind, and without the expectation that such behavior will grant us special privilege or a "get out of jail free" card. For reward to be a facet of relationship rather than a transaction, it must be a gift, not an investment; it must be given away free and clear, not as a loan to be paid back with interest.

If we develop a right perspective on influence, submission, and reward—and combine it with a solid foundation of communication and trust and an open door of cooperation and forgiveness—we will place ourselves in the best possible position to execute our followership with excellence and to see organizational goals advanced through our involvement. We turn next to considering a few of the specifics we can anticipate as benefits of our well-developed relationship with our leader.

18

WHAT THE RELATIONSHIP CAN ACHIEVE

As we continue the exploration of our leader-follower relationship, we must remember that the relationship itself is a facet of our followership, and not simply an avenue for achieving desirable outcomes. While we do want to achieve our common purpose, we want to avoid thinking of other people merely as a means to an end.

With that caveat, let's identify some of the possible outcomes we may see as a result of pursuing a healthy relationship with our superiors. Some of these results are highly desirable, but optional—such as balance, additional opportunities, and job satisfaction. But we *must* cultivate other results—such as effectiveness and personal development—to be successful.

As followers, we make essential contributions to our organization in the form of our talents, abilities, gifts, experience, and perspective. Once we have established a well-founded relational dynamic with our leaders, we can help them keep a balance in their leadership. As we work from a healthy pace of output and steer clear of "red-zone living," we'll have the opportunity to influence our bosses toward proper pacing as well.

At the same time, we can also be a safeguard to prevent our leaders from going astray in the exercise of their power, authority, and responsibility. Ira Chaleff reminds us that "leaders rarely use their power wisely or effectively over long periods unless they are supported by followers who have the stature to help them do so."[1] This kind of support—this offering of balance to keep our leaders from wandering into power lust or abuse—is best supplied when we have authentic relationships with our leaders and freedom to speak into their lives. Only then can we provide corrective advice from a place of true care and concern—both for their personal welfare and for the health of our peers and our organization. Leaders who are relationally isolated miss out on the resource of people who can prevent them from veering off the cliff and into personal and corporate oblivion.

We, too, benefit from this relational safety net. When we make mistakes or when we need to risk speaking up on an issue, having a solid connection with our leader can provide a bit of cushion that insulates us from the backlash we might otherwise expect. Again, we don't want to view our relationship simply as a "get out of jail free" card, nor do we want to presume that our association with our leader will fully shield us from any and all consequences of our actions. But when situations become strained

> "The four elements followers want from leaders are authenticity, significance, excitement, and community"
> (*Authentic Followership*, 2).

and difficult, being in relationship with someone who holds responsibility, who understands and knows us, and with whom we communicate openly and regularly, can go a long way in garnering assistance. We will find ourselves in a stronger position when we are more tightly intertwined with others (superior and peers alike) who have joined their fates to our own and who are willing to listen to us and extend forgiveness.

In addition to these "storm shelters," we'll find other new and positive opportunities open to us as a result of our relationship with our leader. For example, I served under a leader who constantly received mass amounts of email (maybe you can relate!). After a year and a half of working with this team leader, we had developed a trusting relationship, and I was able to come alongside and help him to write responses to the messages in his overflowing inbox. To assure I could do this well, my leader gave me access to sensitive information and situations. In this way, I was able to truly ease his burden, but this was possible only because we had established a mutually trusting and open connection.

We don't need to look at relationship development as figuring out how to "date" our boss—how to impress, woo, or charm him or her to be on our side. More often, relationship and trust grow slowly as a result of our faithful and excellent work, our habits of communicating appropriately and serving diligently. Our right responses, cooperation, forgiveness, and submission continually add to creating a healthy foundation.

In 2011, in the wake of the earthquakes and tsunami that struck Japan, I served as part of a disaster relief team. My direct boss, James, was also a part of the team, but the relief effort was actually led by Dean, one of James' other followers who lived in and was well-connected in Japan. Two weeks of laboring long days side by side allowed Dean and I to establish a good connection, even though he was significantly more senior than I was in the organization.

Toward the end of the trip, we had an important meeting with local representatives to establish future responsibility for the relief work. Leaders of various constituencies in Japan attended. As team leader, Dean facilitated this meeting, and surprisingly, he asked me to accompany him. He didn't ask James, his boss who was a far more appropriate figurehead and spokesman than I was.

When I asked Dean why he wanted me—a relative nobody in our organization at the time—he made it clear that he had seen my work over the last two weeks and that he needed what I had to offer at the upcoming meeting. It seemed risky for Dean not to invite James—a choice that could be perceived as an insult. But Dean had such a relationship with James, and had developed a strong enough connection with me, that he could take that risk (which, knowing James, was truly minimal) and get the support he needed to make the meeting as effective as possible. In the end, the outcome of that meeting felt like our team's most significant contribution to establishing long-term relief, even more so than truckloads of rice and supplies that we had delivered over the previous 14 days.

My opportunity to serve alongside Dean was a result of a growing relationship. By serving with excellence and diligence, I created trust and communication within that relationship, which in turn opened a new opportunity for me to serve. Remember that excellence in followership is not *so that* we get preferential treatment or new assignments; rather, fulfilling our role and following well often generate new chances to serve and exercise stewardship.

This notion of sponsorship or advocacy is an incredible relational benefit for us followers. Leaders, by nature of their position, have access to resources, projects, and the ears of others. When you have served faithfully and established a connection with such a leader, she or he is able to recommend, nominate, or assign you to new areas of service. And in these new opportunities you'll find platforms for additional influence—and also for personal growth and job satisfaction.

You may be asked to participate in a project for which you don't feel wholly qualified. In this case, your leader likely recognizes your potential, seeing that you already possess critical characteristics of reliability, honesty, and cooperation. When you're placed in a new situation as a result of your leader's endorsement, you have the opportunity to grow and develop within new circumstances, and perhaps while working alongside new leaders and peers. Relationship with your leader can thus help to ensure that your involvement does not become stagnant.

We can see, then, that another outcome of our relationship with our leader is likely to be our own satisfaction. We'll feel more fulfilled in our jobs if we have meaningful work to do; if we receive the appreciation of our bosses; and if we are given opportunities to influence and be involved. And this feeling of satisfaction usually has the benefit of spurring us on to continue following with excellence, thus creating a cycle of a stronger relationship with our leaders, additional opportunities, greater satisfaction ... and on it goes!

Lest we lose perspective, however, let us recall that ultimately our desire should be effectiveness. Whatever the aims of our organization, whatever our specific tasks, we should seek to make positive contributions—achieving goals, enhancing vision, and rightly embodying core values. We should continually view our relationships with our leaders as a critical factor in becoming more effective within our organization. We, our leaders, and even our peers can all benefit from this environment—and the resulting emphasis on communication, trust, cooperation, forgiveness, balance, safety, sponsorship, growth, and satisfaction.

19

FOLLOWING "POOR" LEADERS

In our journey of seeking to follow well, we tend to think that things would be so much easier if only we had a better boss. Leaders, by nature of their position, tend to be more readily targeted for criticism, and we followers all too often take easy shots at them, identifying their weaknesses and mistakes and holding them responsible, at least in part, for the difficulties we encounter.

But poor leadership is not an excuse for poor followership: "You cannot blame your boss if you are not following well."[1] While our relationship with our leader is a two-way street, we followers bear ultimate responsibility for the way we walk our own paths of service and contribution. In this pursuit, we must guard ourselves from inappropriately labeling and dismissing our superiors as unfit and thus unworthy of being followed.

The reality is that all leaders are poor leaders. While some may use the adjectives "bad" or "incompetent," I prefer to say that every leader is a "poor" leader—impoverished in some way, lacking some ability, skill, knowledge, or characteristic that would enable him or her to lead with greater excellence. After all—I'll say it again—leaders are human too: They inherently lack self-sufficiency, fall a few items short of the complete package, and thus depend—like all of us—on others to come alongside and fill in the missing pieces.

From this frame of reference, calling our leaders "poor" is a qualitative acknowledgment rather than a value judgment. Instead of applying a critical label, we admit that our leaders are incomplete, which should enable us to maintain a proper perspective when we face difficulties in following well under their authority. We must realize that people are not inferior because they lack something; those who are financially poor are not lesser human beings because they are impoverished. Acknowledging the state of poverty that exists in each of us— including ourselves, our coworkers, and our leaders—and across our organization should motivate us to be all the more intentional about following well, recognizing our value and the necessity of our contribution, and then offering what we have to fill in where others are lacking. At the same time, our journey of personal development should help us to see where *we* are poor and prompt us to look to others for the support we need. Here we see that the cooperation discussed earlier is not just for the sake of synergy and efficiency, but is actually a necessity, owing to the truth that we are all poor in some regard.

This paradigm of poverty should also encourage us to contemplate how we may be contributing to an environment of less-than-perfect leadership. Barbara Kellerman, author of *Bad Leadership: What It Is, How It Happens, Why It Matters*, affirms that "bad leaders depend absolutely on bad followers to sustain them."[2] Our support of ineffective and unethical people and practices helps to maintain an environment of bad leadership.[3] Our own failings and difficulties in submitting, honoring, and participating can add significantly to the struggles our leaders face in trying to lead well. And our commitment to contribute to the leader-follower relationship should cause us to pause before heavy-handedly doling out judgmental labels against our leaders. In becoming a follower, I have tied myself to my leader's welfare to some degree. Rather than bemoan the poverty, I should step up: I am in the perfect position to address that poverty and to provide support so that my leader's lackings and gaps can be as limited as possible.

James Galvin defines four categories of abusive leaders: Those who are incompetent, disempowering, manipulative, or toxic.[4] While some people do abuse their positions and display their poverty in ways that hurt others, it's important to ask a question before immediately latching onto one of these labels: Is the leader *using* his or her power, or *abusing* it? And Ira Chaleff offers the quick test of honesty and decency: Are these two qualities apparent in the leader's leading?[5] If so, then we must be cautious about dismissing an uncomfortable use of authority as bad leadership. Power used for purposes with which we don't agree is not necessarily a failure of leadership. If we rush to judgmental labels to slough off the reality of the situation, we reveal more about our own poverty than about the quality of our leaders.

Like all of us, leaders face poverty in any number of areas. Although we often presume leaders are visionaries, they may lack a grasp of the full picture or have a limited range of possibilities available to them. Tracey Armstrong writes, "So what if the [leader's] plan is not complete? We see only in part. Never judge your leader for not having the whole picture."[6] Instead, we should seek what we can supply to enhance our leaders' visions, and enable them to see better, farther, and more clearly. Perhaps we can offer perspective, counsel, or listening ears. At the least, we can extend understanding and grace, as we remember our leaders are still in process, developing needed competencies in vision and planning.

Leadership poverty may reveal itself in the absence of a particular skill, ability, knowledge, or expertise. While we may wish that our leaders would be the best at every aspect of every job we perform as their followers, the reality is that our leaders have their own set of experiences and talents. Because they may not be as accomplished as we are in a particular area, we have an excellent opportunity to follow well by getting involved in tasks that match our suite of abilities. By doing so, we free our leaders from having to invest heavily in areas of weakness and instead allow them to focus on strengths or other areas that are not so readily fulfilled by other followers. A team exists because there is a need for a variety of skills and knowledge, and we should not be surprised when we discover that our leaders are in need of skills that we can provide.

Leadership can often be lonely, isolating, discouraging, and burdensome. It's not reasonable to expect that leaders should always be able to buck up and hang in there; that expectation denies their humanity. Leaders, just like followers, are not self-sufficient islands; all need help, encouragement, and connection from others to thrive. Even those of us who do quite well working alone often need affirmation and a sense of the bigger picture.

Once we acknowledge the reality of these emotional and interpersonal struggles, we shouldn't be surprised when a leader needs a listening ear to help in handling this sphere of poverty. Whether that support takes the shape of formal counseling by a licensed practitioner or regular contact with a mentor or confidant, we as followers should validate our leaders' courage as well as the legitimacy of their need for this level of communication and companionship. "Some people see a leader's need for therapy or counseling as calling the leader's fitness for office into question. This attitude is a terrible disservice to our leaders and ourselves. It denies our leaders tremendous growth opportunity, and it denies us the benefit of self-examined leadership."[7]

Of course, leaders experience poverty in many other areas. As we have discussed, one of the results of a healthy leader-follower dynamic should be that we gain clarity about the particular areas in which our leaders lack and seek ways to discern how we can be part of their support networks. In doing so, we positively affect our leaders, our fellow followers, and the organization as a whole.

Once we've gained a right perspective on poor leadership and an awareness of our leaders' areas of poverty, how should we respond so as to continue in excellent followership? James Galvin surfaces a number of possible responses—most of which are negative, such as avoiding leadership or perpetuating the cycle of abuse.[8] Let's concentrate instead on the helpful ways we can address the poverty in our midst.

We have already explored many ways we can contribute within an environment of less-than-ideal leadership. We should serve, support, and supply. We must remember that to hold back on using our skills both harms and deprives the team. In discovering our leaders' areas of poverty, we may come face to face with the very reason we are a part of this group; how sad it would be to miss out on the opportunity to make a significant difference in fulfilling a common purpose! We cannot let misplaced expectations, assigning blame, skirting responsibility, or the ease of targeting leadership undermine our wholehearted engagement with these unique chances to exert influence.

> "You will not be able to work with the limitations or imperfections in your leadership if you don't walk in love towards them" (*Discovering Followership*, 83).

Other healthy responses to the reality of poverty include operating from a place of pre-forgiveness and embracing a habit of active forgiveness. But how long should this last? In the wake of repeated errors and failings, at what point do we give up on forgiveness? Aside from legal, ethical, or blatant abuse situations, the answer to that question primarily depends on you. When you can no longer be supportive of your leader, when you can no longer submit and honor, then you've reached the end of forgiveness. But this choice to cease forgiving brings about another end as well: your involvement in that particular department, project, or organization. If your leader has broken the law, violated ethical standards, or caused harm, he or she should go—the question is not really one of forgiveness. However, when the issue surrounds an ongoing interaction with a "poor" leader, we cannot withdraw our support and involvement unless we also withdraw from the situation. We can, and perhaps should, make our concerns known, but if we choose to remain in a situation while also forswearing any intention of submitting to that leader, we act contrary to excellent followership. To stay when all we have to offer is opposition, insubordination, and criticism can only be harmful and infectious, and we will no longer be able to make a positive impact. Keeping ourselves involved only to serve as an obstruction to the leader prevents us from fulfilling our followership obligations.

Author Jimmy Collins refers to this move as "firing your boss." He writes, "Either get on board and support the boss or fire him."[9] Interestingly, this move does not mean that you can eject your boss from your organization; more often, you'll have to remove yourself and find a new leader under whom you can follow well. A deep-seated place in you may insist, "I'm not the problem so why should I have to leave?" The truth, however, is that if you cannot continue to forgive and support—and if your leader has not violated legal or ethical standards, or abused power or position so as to harm others—then the problem actually is with you. If you cannot submit to and support a leader in his or her impoverished state—whether we label that incompetence, ineptitude, or idiocy—then it's time for you to go. I urge you to make these considerations *after* pursuing a healthy relationship with your leader, after attempting to make a positive contribution to his or her journey of personal development, and after making appropriate use of other feedback mechanisms to share your awareness of your leader's needs with others who may be able to help.

If you must make this move—and many authors listed in the "Further Reading" section discuss this step—do not do so under the illusion that you'll be able to find a new situation with a better leader. Whatever attributes or virtues your next leader may have, he or she will also be a poor leader, and you too will still be a poor follower (as we all are!). I encourage you to never give up on intentionally engaging in your own personal development, and don't allow yourself to fall back to an inaccurate perspective on the humanity of your leader.

Part 5

FOLLOWERSHIP IN RELATIONSHIP WITH OTHER FOLLOWERS

As followers, we necessarily have some sort of dynamic with a leader, but we have other connections too. In most cases, we are not the only one following a particular leader—we have fellow followers. To follow with excellence, we must consider our relationship and interaction with our peers. If we ignore them, we limit our opportunities for influence and contribution, and if we focus solely on our relationship with our leader, we may be accused of looking out only for ourselves, trying to gain preferential treatment and establish connections to promote our own well-being and influence. By coming alongside our peers, we add another layer of authenticity and trust in demonstrating our ultimate commitment to the association's common purpose—in contrast to our own career building and self-interest.

20

ASSOCIATION

When we become part of a group, we make a significant decision in choosing to serve under the responsibility and oversight of a leader. Much of that significance stems from the reality that, by associating ourselves with an organization, we may need to change or adapt our perspectives or behaviors. True enough, we sometimes join organizations because we specifically desire the personal impact and growth that will result from our experiences and involvement with this particular collection of people, who share a certain interest, aim, or identity. Regardless of whether this is our purpose, we must consider the effect of association if we are to follow well.

At the most basic level, associating ourselves with some group endeavor means we are joining something. We are choosing to align ourselves with a community that has some definition or goals. While any group is a collection of individuals, it is also more than that. Common bonds—whether many or few—unite a group and supersede the variety of personalities and perspectives represented by each person. If we associate ourselves but resist subordinating our individual desires for the good of the group, we condemn ourselves to a poor followership experience from the outset.

One organization that I have worked with has a very specific policy that women were permitted and welcomed to serve in any role, at any level of leadership. The core documents that all new members were expected to read and affirm stated this policy clearly. So it both baffled and disturbed me when someone joined the organization who held an opposing view. Why would he choose to join the organization, knowing that he disagreed with a segment of the organization's very DNA? Even worse, he joined a team that was headed by a woman leader; he made this choice—he wasn't forced or placed into this particular situation. This woman leader soon accepted a promotion to become senior leader of the entire geographic region in which this new member was involved. If he had any expectation that his differing viewpoint would somehow be a non-issue, something that wouldn't actually affect his day-to-day involvement with the organization, he couldn't have been more wrong.

The team and the wider area experienced a season of turmoil, in part because of the deeply held, misaligned values that this member would raise time and time again. After several years (!) and much strife for both his leader and his teammates, he made the only move left to him: He resigned from the organization entirely.

I was involved in this situation from a distance, and the experience underscores for me the weight of association. Joining a group means establishing a connection with other people, and it requires a degree of conformity and submission. If we join an organization while holding diametrically opposing viewpoints, perhaps expecting that they will be inconsequential or that the organization will ultimately change its perspective to accommodate our own, we start with an unwise and unrealistic expectation.

During my university days, I was a member of an on-campus fraternity. Although it was not a specifically Christian organization, as with many such Greek-letter societies in the United States, its mid-19th-century founders were of the Christian faith. As a result, there was Christian vocabulary and symbolism sprinkled amid the traditions and language. I was somewhat shocked to witness the display of ignorance that erupted when some new members of differing faith backgrounds so ardently opposed these Christian trappings that they actually performed acts of vandalism in an effort to blot out the traces of Christian imagery. What I found must upsetting was that none of this Christian imagery or tradition had been hidden from them when they considered joining the fraternity; the targets of their vandalism had been on open display when they first visited, and they were educated in the historical foundations of the society as part of their membership process. Yet somehow they believed that they could join anyway and then set upon a crusade to eradicate the elements that were distasteful to them.

> "Your reason for following may have nothing to do with getting ahead, personal growth, or intellectual development. Instead, it may be about the intimacy and social support that develop when people bond together" (*Power of Followership*, 66).

Although we certainly hope to be an influence for the better within our organizations, we are poor followers if we begin our association with a need to fundamentally rewire the group to make *it* congruent with *our* values. Change often does happen from the inside out, but when we oppose quintessential elements of an organization's values, goals, or methods, we would be wise to rethink our choice to join. Under such circumstances, even when we believe we could make improvements in the operation, we're more likely to be destructive than helpful. In such cases, joining is probably more ego-driven. We should instead seek to see the common purpose achieved, and to contribute to the creation of an environment that will enable everyone—not just us—to apply themselves in the best way possible.

As we talked about in Chapter 5, followers do have an obligation to submit to their leaders. But likewise followers must also submit to the group. If we are to honor our obligation to participate with excellence and authenticity, we must be willing to shape ourselves so that we are sufficiently aligned with the group. Only then can we be contributing members and not fractious, internal antagonists.

Associating with any group means that our membership becomes a part of our identity. Whether we say, "I work for ... " or "I am a volunteer at ... " or "I am a member of ... ," this association becomes representative and descriptive of who we are. And therefore, it's disingenuous for someone to say he is a member of an organization that values women in leadership while personally believing the opposite. Whatever membership formalities we undertake, if we don't agree on the association's values, then we are wrong to characterize ourselves as being a part of a particular organization.

Of course not every member must be a carbon copy of every other member, but effectiveness does require some basic level of overlap in perspectives and aims. Many organizations publish a document enumerating their core values—the essential characteristics that describe the organization and those to which every member should be willing and able to give assent. Even if we aren't equally excited about each core value, at a minimum we should not feel any fundamental disagreement or resistance to these values. If we do, it falls upon us as followers to reconsider whether our association is right—both for us and for the group.

21

PEER RELATIONSHIPS

Many of the things we can do to build healthy, effective relationships with our leaders can also be applied in our relationships with our team members, coworkers, and peers. After all, whether we are considering leaders or peers, we are seeking to build cooperative relationship, a dynamic with others that promotes our mutual contributions.

Establishing trust is one of the most crucial aspects of fostering such a relationship. Just as our leader must know that our involvement is not merely selfish manipulation in a bid to improve things for ourselves, so too our coworkers must be assured we are authentic with our comments, actions, and offers of help, and they're not driven merely by a yearning for recognition or career building, nor a desire to diminish or devalue others to make ourselves seem more excellent by contrast.

A working relationship based on trust allows everyone involved to set aside the fear and caution that may otherwise cause restraint. When we're sure of others' motive, we can act freely and openly—and with a willingness to serve in a way that is not primarily about benefitting ourselves. When we don't have to spend time and energy protecting ourselves from the schemes of others, we can give more to fulfilling the purpose at hand. If we focus on openness, respect, and forgiveness in our peer relationships, we can communicate—even in difficult conversations—without the effort it takes to skirt certain issues when we don't know how our comments or criticisms will be received. If we trust our peers and they trust us, we can say and do what needs to be said and done, and we'll have a solid foundation for repairing the damage if something is misconstrued, offensive, or hurtful.

Ira Chaleff identifies, in addition to trust, a number of ways that followers relate to one another. He includes "staying alert to the individual needs of each member ... appreciating our differences ... respecting each other's boundaries ... building strong lateral communication and coordination."[1] Each of these is a natural extension of the principles we've identified in pursuing our relationships with our leaders and working on our own personal development.

> "If we don't trust one another, then we aren't going to engage in open, constructive, ideological conflict. And we'll just continue to preserve a sense of artificial harmony" (*The Five Dysfunctions of a Team*, 91).

Navigating cross-cultural dynamics is one particular area in which we can work to better relate to our peers. It's not solely the role of the leader to teach, train, and sensitize others about multicultural issues; every follower can play a valuable role in improving cross-cultural interaction for the group as a whole: "The task of the manager, and indeed the members, of any work group becomes not just to practice cultural intelligence but also to engender and encourage cultural intelligence in all members of the team in their everyday interactions with each other and their overall work for the organization."[2]

As we come to better know ourselves in terms of our needs and healthy boundaries, and as we seek to come alongside our leaders in a supportive way, we should adopt that same perspective with our coworkers as well. Even if our peers haven't undertaken a similar discipline of personal development, we can encourage them as we seek to know and understand them better.

As we follow with excellence, we can provide benefits for our coworkers as well. Contributing to a synergistic environment; modeling honor, submission, and personal development; and displaying the enthusiasm of ownership can become contagious. These positive actions in our own lives can radiate out along the threads of the supporting web-work of which we are a part, encouraging others to act similarly.

On the other hand, if we fail to follow well, we can severely hinder our peers in their following. If we act with an attitude of disrespect, routine nay-saying, or a lack of faithfulness, we create a work environment in which our peers may be unintentionally, but inevitably, drawn into similar behaviors. If we turn the situation into an "every man for himself" dynamic, we almost force our coworkers into the same pattern of self-interested manipulation. Although each of us is responsible for our own actions, we play a significant role in shaping—for better and for worse—the actions and attitudes of others. It often takes only one inappropriately vocal, dissenting member to establish division in what was previously a relatively unified environment. That doesn't mean we should never speak up when we have opposing perspectives, only that we must be mindful that we have the potential to do so in a way that is helpful, or in a way that is harmful.

22

INFORMAL LEADERSHIP

W e may find that our excellent followership leads to opportunities that involve more overt aspects of leadership. Even without a change of title or role, peers may routinely look to us for direction and perspective, and leaders may regularly delegate various areas of responsibility or invite us to join in on important conversations. Where once we were consulted only about our particular areas of expertise, we may begin to find others seeking our opinion on a wider sphere of topics. Those who oversee fundamental issues of values and vision may begin looking to us for our input, asking not only for us to present our own thoughts, but also to represent the perspectives and concerns of our peers.

We might call this expression of followership "informal leadership": fulfilling typical leadership functions without a formalized title, role, or job description. The opportunities to serve in informal leadership roles are born of relationship, proven character, and a record of following well. Robert Kelley identifies a similar concept, which he terms "small-l leadership."[1] In contrast to highly formalized "Big-L leadership," Kelley writes, "Small-l leadership is practiced among peers, most often in teams. The degree of success has less to do with the power of a job title than the power of expertise, a credible reputation, influence, and persuasion."[2]

If we have these characteristics, our followership will likely grow in the direction of informal leadership. We should remind ourselves, however, that leadership—whether formal or informal—doesn't have to be a personal goal. Rather, as we focus on following with excellence, and in combination with our own unique résumé of abilities and characteristics, we may find such informal leadership (and perhaps formal leadership as well) becoming part of our contribution. If and when these opportunities do arise, we want to be prepared to continue our trajectory of following well even as the specific avenues for doing so change over time.

> "Informal leaders arise because their ideas or behavior are well received by others and because they practice good communication skills in putting their ideas across" (*Cultural Intelligence*, 123).

Kelley identifies four characteristics of the "small-l leader": influence, expertise, persuasion, and credibility. The notion of influence has been a continuous thread throughout our look at followership, from dismantling misconceptions to evaluating our relationships with our leader and peers. Influence is likely to be a continuous aspect of an excellent follower's following, but the spheres of that influence will vary as our relationships and the needs of the project or organization develop. Expertise is also a core characteristic of an excellent follower, as we steward our talents and knowledge, and as we continue to grow.

However, you may feel intimidated by the characteristic of persuasion. Maybe your feelings are similar to my own: Although I feel I can make my point in a conversation, I would hardly describe myself as persuasive—especially once I compare myself with those who clearly have this skill. But as I think about followership and informal leadership, I realize that persuasion is primarily about communication—yet another frequent topic of our exploration. Being a persuasive communicator includes, in large part, the ability to communicate appropriately: to know what to say and how to say it. It's not solely about our innate charisma or personality. From this perspective, all of us who desire to follow well should be working on our persuasive communication; that is to say, we should be developing our ability to communicate successfully and appropriately whether we are offering opinions, criticism, ideas, or support.

Credibility is perhaps one of the most valuable commodities for anyone who is intent on following well. Credibility begins with trust, but it also includes the nuances of expertise, wisdom, and reliability. Someone who is haphazard with their words and inconsistent in their actions will not be considered credible. Even a flare of genius or a flash of innovation—though perhaps praiseworthy—will not beget a lasting reputation for credibility.

In considering credibility and reputation, then, Tracey Armstrong asks this simple question: "Is there anyone in your organization who can validly speak negatively of your name?"[3] Since much of our formal evaluation comes exclusively from our superiors, this question is best addressed by considering our broader association with the organization as a whole, especially our peer relationships. Are we following well, not just in ways that will win the approval of our leaders, but with such a quality, consistency, and selflessness that will also garner the respect and appreciation of our fellow followers? Do we serve and support in ways that benefit others but remain unseen by the authority figures? Or, on the flipside, do we hinder or discourage our peers, even if such behavior doesn't show up in a formal quantitative evaluation? Are we manipulative, dismissive, egotistical, deceitful, or territorial, such that our coworkers have a hard time believing we are truly team players who are concerned with the bigger picture, and not just our own agenda?

Establishing credibility and a solid reputation—which may open the doors for informal leadership—is a time-consuming effort. We can't build our consistency, reliability, and trust with one-off interactions. Rather, Kelley says, "the small-l leader who bonds with coworker followers by slogging through the daily project grind and sharing late-night pizzas while meeting deadlines earns more loyalty and credibility than even the most charismatic big-L boss."[4] A credible reputation can thus be a fundamental aspect of our relationship with other followers, but we cannot assume that mere time or seniority will bring it about.

Such an expectation can actually lead to conflict and competitiveness. When a person with less time in the organization is invited into a meeting, offered an assignment, or entrusted with responsibility, do we take note of their reputation, credibility, trust, and relationship? Or do we instead turn our thoughts and feelings to injustice, swearing that he or she must have made some incredible political move to upstage us and achieve this preferred place of followership? Some of our peers may indeed play such games to gain recognition, but on such occasions we should take the opportunity to ask ourselves where we stand in our relationships with our peers and if we are following—especially in this area of peer interaction—as well as we thought we were.

For those of us who are dubious about the quality of our following, we can sometimes find validation and encouragement by acknowledging the opportunities we have for informal leadership. Again, I'm not saying that such leadership should be the goal, nor should we expect it as a reward for following well, but having opportunities to exert such influence can provide a tangible marker of our value within an organization. Effective informal leadership says much more about the excellence of our followership than having a specific job title or even gaining a promotion. Such formal organizational moves can be motivated by other factors, but the invitation and acceptance of both horizontal (toward one's peers) and vertical (toward one's leaders) influence is very hard to pin on anything except the credibility of one's reputation and service.

If we are presented with an opportunity for informal leadership, how can we be good stewards? Returning to our spiderweb analogy, as followers we work together with companion threads to provide support to our leaders and also to the aims, effectiveness, and survival of our groups. Although all threads contribute to a supporting role, there are some—anchoring threads—upon which many others depend and which thus exert a special aspect of influence. Disturbing a random interior thread of a spiderweb will cause only minor disruption; the spider may not even move immediately to repair it. But if one of the three or four anchor threads is broken, endangering the web's suspension in mid-air, the collapse creates a tangle of many threads, and the spider responds quickly.

We can think of seasons of informal leadership—perhaps a specific assignment or project, rather than a new permanent role in the organization—as cycles that rotate us in (and out) of one of these anchor-thread positions. We have the opportunity and responsibility to continue performing well so that the threads directly connected to us, and to even more remote parts of the web, can continue to fulfill their roles with excellence. But we do not have license to become lax, nor should we boast. Rather, informal leadership offers us a chance to serve our peers in new ways.

Although followership always encompasses our involvement with both our leader and with our coworkers, opportunities for informal leadership can take us into new territory as an advocate for and caretaker of our peers. Being "in the trenches" alongside our fellow followers gives us a perspective on the realities of struggles and opportunities to which our leaders may not have access. Coupled with an opportunity to influence, this means that we may be able to encourage changes that will truly lead to a more effective and encouraging environment for those threads in the organizational network that have previously been overlooked or misunderstood.

Robert Kelley observes that managers do not always successfully allocate or delineate responsibilities and tasks among team members.[5] At times, structures and methods suggested (or imposed) by those with formal leadership authority do not align with the reality—the needs and challenges represented by the members involved. In such a situation, the follower with an informal leadership invitation can suggest and perhaps implement the kinds of allocations, dynamics, and expectations that will enable his or her peers to work effectively. As a trusted counselor and confidant of both one's peers and one's leaders, such a follower can provide a unique role in translating the concerns of one to another in a way that can be heard, received, and responded to, brokering an alignment and understanding that was never before achieved. Michael Useem refers to such intermediaries, saying, "They are not executive assistants, mechanically executing what the boss wants, nor are they grassroots advocates, simply voicing what the people want. Rather, they serve a thinking, translating, and mediating function, transforming what each wants into what all should achieve."[6]

> "This individual is also someone who courageously supports and holds accountable their leader, and other team members, through their acts of selflessness, integrity, and their own capacity to lead" (*Leadership-Followership 360°*, 47).

It is certainly possible that our informal leadership roles may eventually lead to a specific, formalized leadership role—a more permanent opportunity and responsibility to apply our influence, wisdom, skills, and perspective across a segment of the organization and over our peers. But even with such a transition, we should not cease to follow with excellence.

Part 6

FOLLOWERSHIP IN RELATIONSHIP AS A LEADER

W e conclude our exploration of what it means to follow well by examining how to fulfill a leadership role from the perspective of our followership journey. This section on leadership isn't last because leadership is somehow the culmination of followership (look back at Chapter 2), but because having a formal leadership role is only one part of how we can serve with excellence, and it isn't necessarily a part of everyone's journey. If you eventually (or currently) have such a role, you may find it difficult to keep in mind all of the facets of excellent followership we have touched on in the preceding pages. In the midst of managing others, decision-making, and tending to a broad sphere of relationships and responsibilities, you must pay extra attention to the quality of your own followership because there are so many other demands vying for your time and energy. If you have a formal leadership position, then part of your task is to manage yourself as both a follower *and* a leader. These are not mutually exclusive tasks, but to execute both with excellence does require an ever-greater degree of intentionality. In this section we'll explore how to hold onto the truths and perspectives that we've developed as followers, bring them to the forefront, and apply them if we do decide to take on a leadership role.

23

A PERSPECTIVE ON LEADERSHIP

"The essence of leadership is helping people follow well."[1] With these words, James Galvin summarizes and concludes his parable on leading and following with excellence. Among the myriad duties, responsibilities, and opportunities that are part of leadership, "leadership is primarily about relationship"[2] and perhaps the most significant relationship in which a leader should invest is with his or her followers. Since followers are essential and valuable to every organization, followership guru Robert Kelley goes so far as to say, "The ultimate test of leadership is the quality of followers."[3]

As we look at our leadership from the perspective of followership, we cannot ignore this realm of stewardship, of doing what we can to promote others' efforts at following well. What was once an opportunity for us as fellow followers becomes more of a fundamental responsibility if we move into a formal leadership role. We must not deceive ourselves into believing that having a title is primarily for our own benefit; rather, having a leadership role positions us to be a primary resource to those who continue in their followership roles.

As leaders, how do we encourage excellence in followership? We begin by examining our own followership journey. As we think back on misconceptions, obligations, contributions, resources, rest, and personal development, what contributions from our leaders helped (or would have helped) us to fully embrace these aspects of our own followership? What opportunities, encouragements, freedoms, guidance, resources, permissions, or conversations with or from our leaders were beneficial?

Answering this question can be a great exercise in humility; it can help us realize that we haven't gotten where we are—in terms of position, satisfaction, expertise, or relationship—solely through our own efforts. And once we can identify our leaders' affect on our journeys, we can then commit to be and do those things for our own subordinates. There is significant truth to the statement, "If you know how to follow well, then you know what good followers need,"[4] and yet there is an aspect that is incomplete. Although it's great to model our leadership on our own followership experience, it's also important to simply ask our followers what it is they need from us. With this approach, we actually respond to the people whom we serve rather than merely responding to the expectations of our roles.

> "Great leaders achieve greatness because they intentionally surround themselves with people who support, advise, and successfully execute plans" (*Creative Followership*, xviii).

What if your subordinates can't articulate what kind of support they need? Herein lies yet another opportunity: Encourage them to grow, reflect, and become more self-aware, just as you have done (and continue to do). Start by modeling your own good followership. The workplace experience we provide does much to shape our followers' future leadership.[5] And since "followers also watch how their leaders follow their leaders,"[6] we do much to shape our followers' activity and perspective through the ongoing display of our own followership.

Here we'll find significant opportunity for self-evaluation; as Hofstede points out, "If you want to know how your subordinates see you, don't try to look in the mirror; that just produces wishful thinking. Turn around 180 degrees and face your own boss."[7]

Whatever culture we're in—whether another nation or a new office—a primary skill for learning what's appropriate and how to be successful is to observe the natives. Your followers will look to your own interactions with your superiors to find their cue to interacting with both you and their peers. Although much of this interaction may take place behind closed doors, beyond your subordinates' view, your opportunity to live as an example should be an encouragement to "invite in" (a concept we will explore shortly).

We as followers bear responsibility for our followership; serving under poor leaders or alongside difficult peers does not mitigate our role in following well. At the same time, leaders do significantly influence the workplace and the team dynamics, and this, too, affects our ability to follow well. In *Leadership-Followership 360°*, Jef Williams states, "Good followership hinges on whether leadership will allow it to exist."[8] Although as leaders we're not ultimately responsible for the choices our followers make, we can do much to influence followership, for good or bad.

24

DISPLAYING DEPENDENCE

A surefire way to stifle excellent followership is to present ourselves as self-sufficient leaders who are independent of any real need of others' contributions. All of the relational considerations outlined in previous chapters will be immediately swept away if we, as leaders, disavow dependence on others. If we don't acknowledge the necessity of our followers' skills, perspectives, and insights, we seriously hamper their ability to honor and respect us, and we certainly won't encourage them to go above and beyond their basic obligations.

A healthy and productive leader-follower relationship requires a mutual flow of interaction rather than a one-sided demonstration of obedience and submissiveness. When a leader is truly working among his or her followers—no matter the differences in specific tasks—what follows is a sense of being bound to one another in a mutually beneficial, synergistic way. Keeping yourself detached and unavailable, behind a closed door, with an overfull calendar and an overflowing email inbox will only motivate your followers to figure out how to make things work without you. The unreachable boss soon becomes the unnecessary one, and while the team may yet continue to function, it will be deprived of the connections, resources, and perspective that its leader should be contributing.

Instead of detachment, demonstrate dependence. But how can you open yourself to a degree of input and relationship in way that doesn't undercut your future ability to say hard things and make difficult decisions? How can you "be the boss," and make calls that may not be well-received? If you reveal your weaknesses, your own "poverty" and consequent dependence on the abilities of others, will you lose the respect of your followers and your authority? Larry Hirschhorn asks the question this way: "If I ask questions that suggest I don't know what I am talking about, will I lose the respect of my followers, or will they welcome my openness and my invitation to them to help me?"[1]

> "Power is not granted because of position. Power is obtained through a relationship" (*Follower First*, 106).

Displaying dependence is risky. Relationships are risky, and exposing the truth of your interdependence on others can be challenging. Personality traits and cultural expectations will color the extent and the ways in which a leader can validate his or her dependence on subordinates.[2] Revealing your reliance on others will be inappropriate in some situations, as in a large group or public forum. It may be wise to instead identify an individual or small group with which to share your needs and dependence. And at times you may need to communicate your areas of need as directives or assignments to others, assigning tasks that fill in your gaps. Doing so with integrity and authenticity may be a challenge, but I encourage you to acknowledge your needs and to avoid hiding behind your leadership title.

As with so much of the leader-follower dynamic, relationship is central, and that may require us to reveal varying levels of dependence as our connections with others deepen.

Having a foundation of trust—as well as loyal followers who are committed to honoring, respecting, and submitting to our leadership—is necessary for us to display dependence in a way that is well-received and leads to a positive outcome. However, even if the environment is not yet right for us to be vulnerable about our own state of "poverty," it is essential that we do not deceive ourselves into thinking that we don't need others' support. Regardless of what our personality, culture, organization, or roles may permit, at the very least we can be honest with ourselves about our lack of self-sufficiency and our need to rely on others. Once we face this truth, we can explore how to appropriately express this dependence, and—far more important—solicit the involvement of others.

25

ESTABLISHING THE ENVIRONMENT

Organizations, like nations, have their own cultures, which provide norms for everything from relationships and behaviors to methods and outcomes. However, despite these broad influences, a leader will usually have significant opportunities to affect or even dictate the local operating environment. Therefore leaders have the responsibility to establish a structure and environment that will characterize their teams. As leaders, we cannot be passive about our stewardship of creating the tone, expectations, and permissions for interaction, both between leaders and follower(s) as well as among followers themselves.

I have witnessed more than one culture clash when leaders and team members from different operating environments suddenly find themselves working together. Regardless of whether this new working group was the result of mergers, reassignments, rotations, or structural overhauls, bringing together people with different experiences and expectations of what is normal is sure to create tension, perhaps miscommunication, and even some hurt as well. These differences are not insurmountable, but we must acknowledge and work on them. This doesn't mean the leader can automatically choose to impose whatever environment he or she might prefer. Rather, it means that the leader is responsible for guiding the group through a season of "storming"[1]—of weathering the waves that could shipwreck the team and bringing everyone to a safe harbor of cooperation and understanding.

Working through these tense seasons together and in a healthy manner results in positive changes, including new norms that reflect the new reality of the people who are working together. Instead of insisting on the status quo or defaulting to his or her unique preferences, a good leader should create a new operating environment that includes agreed-upon methods and outcomes. I have personally experienced several leaders who viewed each new change of their immediate staff as the creation of a new version of the team ("Team 2.0"), taking the opportunity to both reevaluate and communicate current norms. While this takes time and energy, the results have been that the newest members can feel fully part of the environment that they have stepped into, and the team as a whole moves forward together.

> "Some people take on a role but lead poorly and then call it servant leadership…. They are passive leaders who excuse their lack of action as servant leadership" (*I've Got Your Back*, 53).

Using some observations from other authors, I'd like to surface a few qualities we should consider as we lead our groups and establish their structures and norms.

"Titles change the entire dynamic of a relationship, creating a new set of rules and limits for expression, openness, and authenticity."[2] Titles truly affect a working environment, but not necessarily for the worse. Oftentimes, titles provide clarity, offering a convenient way to identify who is responsible for what and how people and roles are interrelated. However, titles can also be distracting or inhibiting. If some but not all members have titles, jealousy can erupt, or a damaging stratifi-cation may arise among followers. On the other hand, if every-one is given a title—even those with very similar roles—they can feel fake and meaningless, creating nuances between roles where none exist. Some followers find validation in having a title; it may remind them of the significant contribution they make to an endeavor. For others, titles that are not accompanied by responsibility, authority, or salary may feel empty or patron-izing. Leaders must carefully consider whether titles are appro-priate and/or necessary to establishing the structure of a group.

"Leaders do not empower followers. Rather leaders create structural freedom in which followers can exercise their gifts and abilities."[3] I think Rusty Ricketson's comment here misses the reality a bit; part of the way leaders empower and en-courage excellent followership is by implementing and manag-ing appropriate organizational structures. As we explored back in Chapter 4, structure and hierarchy are not inherently inhibiting. Clear roles combined with clear lines of communication, author-ity, and responsibility can lead to greater freedom and opportu-nities for everyone involved. One tool in creating structure may be the use of titles, but additional structural choices, such as the creation of sub-teams, committees, and task forces—along with corresponding spheres of responsibility—will also affect the followership dynamic. In addition, if you as a leader create ways for communication to go over, around, and outside of your leadership and your group/departmental lines, your followers will be more likely to collaborate. Furthermore, discussion with your own peers and superiors may be vital in determining what structure will be possible and beneficial.

"Being open to subordinates requires a leader to reveal more of his or her 'personhood.' One cannot hide behind the role of leader; instead, one must bring more of one's passions, fears, and values to it."[4] Although each of us has an innate preference or hesitance toward being vulnerable—a preference that is likely to change as we work on our personal development—the degree to which we are vulnerable and come across as "human" will go far in establishing an environment that encourages followers to share similar expressions of thoughts, feelings, and concerns. If you use your leadership title or position as a shield or barrier to create distance between your inner self and your coworkers, you can expect that they'll respond similarly. Although some may argue that emotions are not appropriate for the workplace, to ban them is to risk that other appropriate and valuable contributions will be held back as well. If no one on your team feels free to express their thoughts or feelings, then they likely won't offer ideas, questions, criticisms, brainstorms, and insights because they fear such comments may be part of that "frowned-upon emotional stuff" that doesn't belong in the office. As a leader, you'll have to consider the type of permission and freedom you seek to develop and how to communicate this—both overtly through memos and structures as well as implied through your own level of sharing.

Put simply, don't view your humanity—including your thoughts, feelings, and preferences—as a workplace liability. Rather, your working norms should include some clarity on the level of vulnerability and the appropriateness of displaying passions, values, and fears within your group. Of two primary dimensions of leadership—concern for tasks and concern for relationships—focusing on relationships and their interpersonal dynamics and participation pays great dividends. "Research indicates conclusively and unsurprisingly that relationship-oriented leaders tend to have more satisfied subordinates and that this is true across a range of different cultures."[5]

As a leader, you are uniquely positioned to model and encourage the agreed-upon level of vulnerability and should consider these norms to apply to yourself as well as to your followers; there shouldn't be different expectations for what is appropriate for a leader or follower to share. By no means should you vent all complaints or misgivings to your subordinates, but rather carefully consider the level of vulnerability to display to your followers *and* superiors. If your followers are expected to be vulnerable with you, you should have at least a degree of vulnerability with your own leaders—and likely a significant degree of vulnerability with your followers as well. Otherwise, you'll inevitably send mixed messages about such norms, expectations, and permissions, which may cost you valuable follower contributions.

"Are you prepared to accept and manage the likely short-term process losses of greater diversity in order to benefit from the prospective longer-term process gains?"[6] As you reflect on the reality of working with others who have different backgrounds and perspectives, remember that as a leader you play a primary role in establishing an environment that accepts and benefits from that diversity, rather than being ignorant, judgmental, or wasteful of it. Internationalization alone doesn't guarantee a good or beneficial team experience. There are costs—certainly time and energy—involved in growing through the hurdles presented by cultural variety. You and your team will likely need to adjust expectations, too, especially as you initially adapt to a multicultural reality. You may need to relax deadlines, productivity targets, and other measurables as your team learns how to communicate and cooperate. As the leader, you have the primary role in establishing these expectations and promoting the value of this investment. Short-term frustrations and perceived hopelessness among team members can only be overcome by your encouragement in embracing cross-cultural realities within your group dynamic.

"Submissive leaders are listening leaders."[7] We've already talked quite a lot about submission as an obligation—submission to our leaders, and submission to our fellow followers. But submission does not end when you take on a leadership role. Not only must you submit to your own superiors, but you can also demonstrate submission to your followers. This doesn't mean handing over the reins of responsibility or abandoning your post, but it does mean being open to input from others. At times such submission may require that you come alongside your subordinates' decisions and recommendations, listening to their ideas, lending your support, and even setting aside your own preferences. Submissive leaders acknowledge that the best idea or the most accurate judgment may come from someone without a title.

As you take time to listen to your followers, you establish an environment that values the input of every member. But your listening must be authentic—it must go beyond politeness. A leader's listening encourages dialogue, and dialogue is an opportunity for a group to uncover the very best idea, rather than merely accepting the one that is delivered the loudest or with the most authority. Followers will follow best if they're given a platform to communicate and express themselves, to bring their perspectives and knowledge into the realm of discussion. A good leader will encourage followers to share, and to listen to one another, by exhibiting a willingness to hear and respond to everybody, without preference for those whose seniority or job description might imply privilege.

26

INVITING IN

My first full-time experience as a team member was as part of a regional leadership/support team operating in the Middle East and Central Asia. My role was primarily an administrative one, handling various logistics and details related to communication, calendar, and team management. A few months in, there was a small "admin huddle," a two-day networking opportunity for others like me who were serving in administrative support roles.

As we discussed various aspects of our roles, from sharing which tools and resources we found helpful to designing systems for organizing data and communications, much of our conversation centered around the working dynamic with our leaders. The five of us in attendance all had a sense that our role could become more effective if we could improve the interaction with those we were serving. We all recognized that there were many times our leaders simply didn't know how to make use of us, especially since our skills and strengths tended to be very different from our leaders'. We had each encountered leaders who were hesitant to ask for our involvement or who resisted delegating too much out of a concern for overwhelming us.

We unanimously decided that it would be most helpful to us if our leaders made a regular practice of "inviting us in"— bringing us personally and directly into communication loops, meetings, and even on business trips. Because of the differing perspectives and abilities that existed among us and our leaders, we realized that if we relied solely upon our leaders' abilities to determine strategies and assignments, certain details, needs, and possibilities would always be overlooked. Forcing a visionary leader to identify and articulate specific administrative tasks wasn't leading to an optimal working environment for any of us. One solution was for our leaders to bring us into their circumstances so that we could directly experience and personally apply our own vision to the needs at hand.

As leaders, we carry our own perspectives, abilities, biases, and strengths into our work environment. We also bring significant areas of "poverty," gaps in our understanding, vision, and perception. If we put ourselves in the place of gatekeeper between our workers and the situations at hand, we inevitably filter that situation through our own personal grids, thus what we describe to our subordinates is a distilled version of the actual circumstances. We unknowingly strip out details and information that may be important, facts that may prompt more effective courses of action or that may highlight even more relevant needs. Relying only on our experience of a situation, we will entirely miss some nuances of what's taken place, what's been said, or what's been intended. We will fail to realize all of the implications that may be sparked by a particular event or conversation. Although we do our best to relate the nature of the reality to our followers, we will have lost some pertinent data along the way, and our team members will not be able to respond to the situation as it is, but only to our interpretation of it. Even if the directives and task assignments we make result from consultation with our subordinates, they will ultimately be made in our own image, suffering from our own limitations and weaknesses.

By inviting our followers in, by bringing them personally into the experience alongside us, we also bring in a wider array of strengths and perspectives to a situation, and we lessen the risk that we will miss or misinterpret a vital aspect of that reality. Someone with different gifts and perspective will respond differently than we will. While that difference may create some tension, we are almost assured of getting a more accurate picture of reality and being able to develop a more appropriate course of action as a result. A follower's firsthand experience can help ensure that we make first-rate decisions the first time around.

> "The trade-off for giving people a sense of participation is higher time consumption" (*How to Be a Star at Work*, 199).

Inviting in cannot be done lightly, however. The bringing together of different perspectives does introduce the possibility for tension, which is just one reason that inviting others in can feel more burdensome than helpful. But mature tension can actually be healthy and helpful. To lessen the risk of destructive tension, however, we must establish a foundation of trust within our relationships (as I've mentioned throughout this book). Our own personal development should include opportunities to acknowledge and value interpersonal differences so that when these differences surface, we can channel them into helpful dialogue rather than into divisiveness and dysfunction.

I cannot overemphasize the role of trust within this dynamic of inviting in. Certainly there are occasions when confidentiality precludes a leader from bringing others into a situation, and there are likely many other situations when a leader may be permitted to invite followers in but is hesitant to do so because he or she is not sure how the followers will respond.

After the admin huddle, I did begin to build trust with my leader, and a year and a half later, our relationship was at the point that I was able to assist in drafting email responses to situations that I previously would never even have known about. It was a testimony of my leader's trust in me—a trust that allowed me to offer a new level of service in relieving my leader's workload.

Inviting in does come at a price. It takes energy to build trust, though as a leader and a follower, you are already committed to the value of establishing trust with your superiors, peers, and subordinates. In addition, inviting in will take time and likely financial resources as well: time to brief and debrief, money to bring an additional person along to a conference or meeting. A leader's own trust account may be taxed a bit as he or she may need to persuade superiors that directly involving a follower is the best course of action. Yet even with all of these costs, the benefit of inviting in a wisely chosen, trusted subordinate can be immeasurable. There is no telling what facts or opportunities, what effectiveness or efficiency we may have missed without having his or her unique perspective and presence.

Inviting in increases the value of followers to an organization while also providing followers with new areas of responsibility and new ways to grow and apply their talents. Inviting in also stretches a follower's understanding of submission, honor, and respect—qualities that must be maintained even when it feels like the gap in authority and responsibility between leader and follower may narrow as a result of the follower's more direct involvement. So, too, followers who are invited in will need to wisely manage their relationships with peers who are not invited; the potential for jealousy and perceived favoritism must be intentionally counteracted to ensure that any benefits to the organization are not canceled out by increased disunity within the ranks. Inviting in is a win-win: a follower feels trusted, included, and heard, and the leader gets to take full advantage of all available human resources to pursue the group's goal.

27

EMPOWERING AND PROMOTING

In addition to promoting followership through displaying dependence and inviting in, there is yet another leadership function: turning followers loose! Seeing followers equipped and entrusted to carry out tasks is a necessary and satisfying aspect of leadership. While leaders will likely prefer to have differing amounts of oversight or hands-on involvement, at some level, every leader should want their followers to be able to work independently. Remember, leaders and followers are both necessary, and their work differs; this means that an effective leader will need to provide the resources, relational networks, and freedom that will enable followers to be who they are and to make their particular contributions to the group.

This leadership function can be summarized by the term "empowering." Leaders have access and authority that differs from followers, and yet these assets are essential for followers to be able to fulfill their role with excellence. Empowering means that we take from the power available to us and share it in such a way that followers can grow and work with a greater degree of efficiency. By delegating, setting expectations, granting permission, allocating resources, and brokering relationships, we employ what we have so followers can do what they do.

If we are truly to empower our subordinates, we must be involved enough to know what they need, without stifling or micromanaging. It is a balance of observing and stepping in, of affirming interdependence while granting independence. If we do well in this, we can anticipate our followers' needs and help ensure a ready supply of collaborative networks, guidelines, processes, and raw materials so that followers can work unhindered and uninterrupted. We can then be ready to receive what followers have produced and ensure that it is brought into a place of strategic benefit for the organization as a whole.

Of course, empowering can also be done poorly. It can be used as an excuse for a leader to hide, to cover irresponsibility, laziness, or discomfort with authority. Gene Boccialetti observes, "Many managers who are uncomfortable with managerial authority welcome the current trends in autonomous teams and empowerment. However, they still need to exercise their authority when it is appropriate to do so."[1] An empowering leader should be active and aware, stewarding his or her leadership well. This will enable followers to have what they need, but it will also require the exercise of authority, accountability, correction, and perhaps discipline. In the process of empowering, a leader trains a follower—not necessarily to become a leader, but to become a more excellent follower, employing their gifts and talents while remaining as an honoring subordinate and cooperative teammate.

Empowering is closely linked to another function: promoting. From my perspective, this word has two senses, both of which fit under the broad notion of introducing followers into new spheres of relationship and responsibility. The first is the sense of advertising, which (within this context) I more commonly call sponsorship or advocacy. The second is perhaps the more common workplace notion of granting someone a new position in the organization, which usually includes a broader sphere of influence.

As a result of our own networks and connections, we as leaders have a tremendous opportunity to advertise our followers, to make others aware of their skills and experience. With a broad view of the challenges and needs faced by the organization, we can step in to match those needs with the human resources that can effectively meet them. A good leader will be doing this already within his or her own team or department, but there are likely additional occasions for highlighting a follower in conversation with other leaders. By providing honest assessment and endorsement, a leader can serve as a sponsor, a guarantor of sorts who speaks for the ability and excellence of a follower to meet a need—even one that may be outside of usual responsibilities. In promoting a follower, a leader serves two purposes: providing the larger organization with access to the right (or best) people for the job, and giving followers new opportunities to contribute and connect. Sponsored followers who have the chance to work across the organization gain the benefit of new experiences and meeting new people, as well as a sense of satisfaction and encouragement in being affirmed by their leader.

> "Leaders should participate in the training process instead of outsourcing it" (*Discovering Followership*, 86).

As leaders, we must be conscious never to use such sponsorship as an excuse to "pawn off" an undesirable subordinate onto another team or department. We must sponsor with authenticity, which requires a real sense of the follower's value, along with a true desire to see her or him make the most significant contribution possible. While a permanent transfer is sometimes the wisest course of action for a follower who is in an ill-suited role, as we look at leadership through the lens of followership, what we are aiming at is to recognize followers' value and apply our influence to open doors for their additional involvement and growth.

The second sense of this promoting function is the leader's role in establishing someone in a new position within the organization. Perhaps an empowered, sponsored follower succeeds in such a way that a temporary assignment should be made a permanent role. In another case, a perceptive leader may see that a follower's contribution would be further enhanced if he or she was given formalized responsibility or access to resources. In yet another situation, a leader may discern that other followers will benefit if a particular one of their peers is given line authority.

These promotions cause changes to the organization; they include adjusting the structure and hierarchy so as to enhance the collective working dynamic. Author Patrick Lencioni writes, "[The leader's] job is to create the best team possible, not to shepherd the careers of individual[s]."[2] Again, from our followership lens, we are not looking at promotion as a reward, but rather as a leader exercising his or her leadership as a means to encourage excellent followership and further group effectiveness.

> "The ability to be under authority should drive who emerges as leaders" (*First*, 107; quoting Aubrey Malphurs).

I have observed many situations where one of my peers receives such a promotion, and draws the pity of his or her fellow followers. Numerous leaders that I have spoken to somewhat begrudge their leadership position, primarily because they see it as taking them away from the hands-on, front-line work that they truly loved to do. The burden and stress of an oversight role, the very different kind of responsibility it involves, precludes many leaders from making the life-giving contributions that attracted them to join the group to begin with. Robert Kelley uncovered the statistical reality behind this leadership perspective. "I asked ... leaders how many would go back to their nonleader jobs if they could without a loss of face.

Seventy-five percent said they would." Based on some additional research, he concludes, "Many in leadership positions ... should not be there and do not want to be there."[3]

We must keep this perspective in mind, both as leaders and as followers. As followers, we shouldn't presume that our leaders are currently serving in their most desired position. We must not assume that our leaders feel like they have arrived and are desperate to maintain a stranglehold on their power and title. Instead, we should be moved to appreciate the sacrifices they may be making; they may be setting aside some significant and life-giving work because some other leader believed the bigger picture would be better served if they were in leadership roles.

As leaders, we must carefully weigh any decision to promote someone to a new role and should honestly discuss the ramifications with our followers. Promoting a follower will end his or her current contribution to some degree, and your entire team may significantly feel that loss. In offering a promotion, you may be asking the follower to set aside a role that is well-known and enjoyed. Do not presume that every follower is ultimately aiming for, and will be most satisfied by, a leadership role. But if a follower displays an authentic sense of ownership, a commitment to the common purposes of the group, then you may indeed be able to justify the costs of such a promotion. And it may even turn out that doing so will serve as yet another step— for both of you—in the journey of embracing followership.

FINAL THOUGHTS

No book exhausts its topic. Talking about followership means talking about people and relationship, and there is no end to the facets to be examined, the ideas to be explored. My hope is that this book has provided a framework within which you can consider your own followership, a place to begin as you look for ways to respond well and contribute appropriately within your circumstances. I hope that you have found encouragement and the validation of your worth and of the possibilities for influence that you possess as a follower. And I hope that you have been inspired to commit to following well.

I believe that if we each seek to fulfill our obligations—to participate, steward, honor, submit, and "be" right in our attitudes and intentional about our growth—then our teams, committees, churches, clubs, and organizations could be taken to new places of cooperative achievement and mutually affirming, personally satisfying collaboration. In short, by following with excellence we can experience much more of the value of human community and relationship.

I'd like to conclude with a few quotations that, for me, help to summarize the essence of following well.

"Be aware of being a follower."[1] To follow well, we must be intentional. We must consider who we are and assess our associations and relationships. We cannot delegate the quality of our followership to our leaders, trying to foist responsibility upon them for how we engage and the value of our involvement. As with most processes of personal development, growth in following well requires awareness and investment; if we shrug our shoulders in either hopelessness or indifference, we'll never reach the place where our follower roles become the key to opening the doorway to success at the end of the hall of mediocrity.

"Your purpose in life is always linked to that of another. You can never fulfill or discover your true identity or purpose in isolation. Followership ignites the process of discovering where we fit in the grand scheme of things."[2] Followership is about relationship. As followers, we have a connection to our leaders and to our fellow followers; these connections form a network, a web, and ultimately, a community. That connection can and should be actively developed into a mutually beneficial resource that enables us to serve others and employ our talents and gifts in the realization of our vision and passions, while also providing us with opportunities to embrace the depths of who we are—uncovering the challenges that cause us to struggle as well as life-giving outlets for our involvement and service.

"We are given to think in terms of individuals and individual responsibility ... . But what we tend to ignore is that the beliefs, views, and actions of any individual, including those in leadership roles, can have little effect if those things are not made real, amplified, and extended through the actions of those in follower or subordinate roles."[3] Our roles as followers are vital. Regardless of what messages we may receive from our corporate culture, social notions on the supremacy of individuality, or quips from leadership literature, we have a job to do. We are necessary strands in the web of mutual support and accomplishment. If that's not the case, perhaps we should be following elsewhere, and lending our influence to the development and credibility of some other endeavor or organization.

"He who cares for his master will be honored."[4] In his book *Creative Followership*, Jimmy Collins twice reminds us of this ancient wisdom from King Solomon in the biblical book of Proverbs (27:18). Extending the idea of relationship mentioned just above, we can remind ourselves that looking to the needs of others, which includes submitting ourselves to our leaders, does not make us inferior to others. Followership is an honorable role. It may not always be appreciated by those around us: Peers and leaders who do not understand our perspective may see us as obsequious and believe us to be ultimately self-serving and manipulative. But part of our opportunity to follow with authenticity and excellence is to do so in a way that others begin to value the role we have as steward, influencer, and fellow member. In this way, we can not only contribute to our organization's fulfillment of its aims, but we can also offer an eye-opening paradigm shift to our superiors, subordinates, and colleagues as we model the integrity, value, and honor of following well.

"Following is about knowing God from a different perspective."[5] Finally, followership for me is just one part of my larger personal journey of Christian faith. Honor, submission, stewardship, leadership, relationship, and community are all defined in light of God's creation of me and his purposes for humanity. Being faithful and excellent in my role as a follower allows me to see God at work—in me and in others—in ways that have been truly transformative.

There is a short story by Rudyard Kipling, "The Cat that Walked by Himself," which is included in *Just So Stories*.[6] It talks about the time when humans first domesticated animals. Dog, horse, and cow, each in turn, approach a woman and exchange their services in hunting, labor, and giving of milk for entrance into the humans' cave home and being provided and cared for. But the cat remains apart, insisting on going his own way and being tied down to nothing. In the end, when the cat manipulatively gains entry into the cave, he discovers that he is not fully accepted into the community like the dog, horse, and cow are. He performs his jobs of catching mice and entertaining the baby, but he forever bears the animosity of the man and the dog, who promise to throw things and chase him for "always and always and always."

This story has long spoken deeply to me. The cat prided itself on its independence, arrogantly asserting that it was tied to no one and nothing and could do as it liked. Time and again the cat refused to enter the cave in companionship, and in the end, although he does his work and receives his reward of milk, he is never fully accepted as a beloved member of the household like First Friend (the dog), First Servant (the horse), and Giver of Good Food (the cow). The independence on which the cat prides himself becomes the independence that forever limits his relationships and quality of life.

As followers—a role that all of us fulfill in some way or other —I believe we have the opportunity to achieve the fullness of who we were made to be when we engage willingly and intentionally in group endeavors. When we become a contributing member of a community in which we offer what we have for the common good, we also receive the things that we need—including social, spiritual, and emotional nourishment—from those who similarly care about us. True enough, this is a grand vision for most offices and committees, and yet I think that we can indeed head in this direction, embracing the fullness of our followership and gaining a larger vision of who we are meant to be.

PARTICIPATE!

Followership is a lifelong journey—one which I am interested in continuing to learn about and grow into. I'm committed to further challenging myself toward excellence both in my obligations and in my opportunities as a follower.

Your perspective on the ideas in this book and your own experience of followership would be yet another resource from which we could all benefit. Please share your thoughts, questions, comments, and suggestions with the rest of us! Are you a non-American or non-Western reader? Your perspective could be invaluable in shaping followership ideas that apply in cross-cultural situations.

Engage via the book's Facebook page (www.facebook.com/EmbracingFollowership), post a review on Amazon.com or Goodreads, or chime in on Twitter or email. Your words may be the key to unlocking encouragement and insight for others, in much the same way that the quotations from other authors have shaped my own thinking and response. Remember: Excellent followers participate! Be a good steward of the time you spent reading this book and of the unique experiences that have composed your own followership, and share your perspective with the rest of us, that we might all be well-resourced to offer our very best contributions to the groups we belong to and to the people—both leaders and peers—we work with.

SOURCES

For my reflections on many of these books, see my reviews online at Goodreads and Amazon.com.

Anonymous. *Embracing Obscurity*. Nashville: B&H, 2012.

Armstrong, Tracey. *Followership*. Shippensburg, PA: Destiny Image, 2010.

Bjugstad, Kent, Elizabeth C. Thach, Karen J. Thompson, and Alan Morris. "A Fresh Look at Followership: A Model for Matching Followership and Leadership Styles." *Journal of Behavioral and Applied Management* 7, no 3 (2006): 304-19.

Boccialetti, Gene. *It Takes Two*. San Francisco: Jossey-Bass, 1995.

Chaleff, Ira. *The Courageous Follower*. San Francisco: Berett-Koehler, 2009.

Collins, Jimmy, with Michael Cooley. *Creative Followership*. Decatur, GA: Looking Glass Books, 2013.

Edwards, Gene. *A Tale of Three Kings*. Carol Stream, IL: Tyndale House, 1992.

Elmer, Duane. *Cross-Cultural Servanthood*. Downers Grove, IL: InterVarsity Press, 2006.

Galvin, James C. *I've Got Your Back*. Elgin, IL: Tenth Power Publishing, 2012.

Goffee, Rob and Gareth Jones. *Authentic Followership*. Boston: Harvard Business School Press, 2007.

Gorton, Dennis L. with Tom Allen. *Leading the Followers by Following the Leader*. Camp Hill, PA: Christian Publications, 2000.

Hanif, Rahmat, Samra Tariq and Neelam Yousaf. "Reciprocity between Followership & Servant Leadership—Moderating Effects of Attributes." *Social Science Research Network* (March 27, 2013). http://ssrn.com/abstract=2240355.

Hirschhorn, Larry. *Reworking Authority*. Cambridge, MA: MIT Press, 1997.

Hofstede, Geert. *Cultures and Organizations*. New York: HarperCollins, 1994.

Imoukhuede, Omokhai. *Discovering Followership*. Chicago: Summit House, 2011.

Jones, Laurie Beth. *The Path: Creating Your Mission Statement for Work and for Life*. New York: Hyperion, 1996.

Kellerman, Barbara. *Followership: How Followers Are Creating Change and Changing Leaders*. Boston: Harvard Business School Press, 2008.

Kelley, Robert E. *The Power of Followership*. New York: Doubleday, 1992.

———. *How to Be a Star at Work*. New York: Three Rivers Press, 1999.

———. "In Praise of Followers." *Harvard Business Review* 66, no. 6 (1988): 142–48.

———. "Rethinking Followership." In *The Art of Followership*, 5–15. San Francisco: Jossey-Bass, 2008.

Lawrence, James. *Growing Leaders*. Peabody, MA: Hendrickson, 2006.

Lencioni, Patrick. *The Five Dysfunctions of a Team*. San Francisco: Jossey-Bass, 2002.

Lingenfelter, Sherwood and Marvin K. Mayers. *Ministering Cross-Culturally*. Grand Rapids: Baker Academic, 2003.

MacLeslie, T. J. *Designed for Relationship*. Seattle: Parvaim Press, 2013.

Rath, G. David. "Comparing Followership with Servant Leadership." Unpublished manuscript.

Ricketson, Rusty. *Follower First*. Cumming, GA: Heartworks, 2009.

Sears, Joanna E. "The Emergence of Implicit Followership Theory." Unpublished manuscript.

———. "Followership Experiences as a Catalyst for Leadership Development: A Qualitative Study." Unpublished manuscript.

Sinclair, Daniel. *A Vision of the Possible*. Colorado Springs: Biblica, 2005.

Smoke, Jim. *Whatever Happened to Ordinary Christians?* Eugene, OR: Harvest House, 1987.

Sumner, Sarah. "The Forgotten Art of Following." *Relevant Magazine* 64 (July–Aug 2013). http://www.relevantmagazine.com/god/forgotten-art-following.

Sweet, Leonard. *I Am a Follower.* Nashville: Thomas Nelson, 2012.

Thomas, David C. and Kerr Inkson. *Cultural Intelligence: Living and Working Globally.* San Francisco: Berrett-Koehler, 2009.

Useem, Michael. *Leading Up.* New York: Crown Business, 2001.

Williams, Jef. *Leadership-Followership 360°.* O'Fallon, IL: JefWilCo Publishing, 2011.

ABOUT THE AUTHOR

Since 2006, Allen Hamlin has served with an international Christian non-profit organization. In this role, he has primarily provided team development training and consultation, along with mentoring and member care, to multiethnic teams serving around the world. He and his wife, Lindsay, have lived in Europe, the Middle East, and Asia. They currently live in Wales, where Allen provides leadership and support for a number of teams operating in southern England, Wales, and Ireland. Both Allen and Lindsay have a deep appreciation for the values and tensions associated with serving in and alongside cultures outside of one's country of origin. They also thrive when they can serve in roles that bring them alongside a leader and vision.

You can reach Allen on Facebook, Twitter (@AllenHamlinJr), and at about.me/allenhamlinjr.

ENDNOTES

Introduction
1. See Sinclair, *A Vision of the Possible*, 170.
2. Robert Kelley, "Rethinking Followership," in *The Art of Followership* (San Francisco: Jossey-Bass), 6.
3. Anonymous, "Embracing Definition," chap. 2 in *Embracing Obscurity* (Nashville: B&H, 2012).
4. Leonard Sweet, *I Am a Follower* (Nashville: Thomas Nelson, 2012), 211.

Chapter 1: A Primer on Followership
1. Robert Kelley, *The Power of Followership* (New York: Doubleday, 1992), 21.
2. A strong notion of followership within Judaism has also been described, and examples from the Hebrew Scriptures have also informed my own journey of followership, as I relate in Chapter 7. See "Judaism: Covenant & Conversation: Followership," *Arutz Sheva*, April 24, 2014, http://www.israelnationalnews.com/Articles/Article.aspx/14889#.U1--9IFdUig.
3. Jim Smoke, *Whatever Happened to Ordinary Christians?* (Eugene, OR: Harvest House), 11; emphasis mine.
4. Sweet, *I Am a Follower*, 21; Rusty Ricketson, *Follower First* (Cumming, GA: Heartworks, 2009), 11

Part 1: Misconceptions and Realities of Followership
1. Several books address the relevance of followership as a topic for investigation, highlighting current trends in business and culture that

have been fueled by the prevalence of the Internet, speed of communication, and emergence of the knowledge economy and "brain-powered worker." My aim here is not to prove that followership is worthy of consideration, but to identify the stereotypes and tendencies that have served to divert our energy and attention from considering the follower role as a primary avenue for our identity and contribution within our various organizations, communities, and associations.

Chapter 2: Followership According to Followers

1. Laura Wisniewski, "All Nurses Are Leaders." *Nursing Link*, accessed December 20, 2013, http://nursinglink.monster.com/benefits/articles/7519-all-nurses-are-leaders.

2. Omokhai Imoukhuede, *Discovering Followership* (Chicago: Summit House, 2011), 93.

3. Tracey Armstrong, *Followership* (Shippensburg, PA: Destiny Image, 2010), 12.

4. Ira Chaleff, *The Courageous Follower* (San Francisco: Berett-Koehler, 2009), 5.

5. Kelley, *The Power of Followership*, chap. 4.

6. Of tremendous personal benefit to me in this journey has been the paradigm of the enneagram, which helped me to identify my tendency to disengage and avoid handling unsatisfactory situations and instead to invest the energy in voicing my personal opinion and preferences. You can find more about this tool in Chapter 11 "Resources for Personal Development."

7. Chaleff, *The Courageous Follower*, 19.

8. Chaleff, *The Courageous Follower*, 24.

9. Michael Useem's book, *Leading Up* (New York: Crown Business, 2001), contains a number of detailed historical case studies that portray the severe implications of followers who fail to recognize that they are not only able, but that it is also their responsibility, to exert influence up the chain of authority.

10. I'm indebted to Robert Kelley, *The Power of Followership*, chap. 2, for surfacing this observation.

11. Armstrong, *Followership*, 148.

Chapter 3: Followership According to Leaders

1. Barbara Kellerman, *Followership* (Boston: Harvard Business School Press, 2008), xx.

2. Jimmy Collins with Michael Cooley, *Creative Followership* (Decatur, GA: Looking Glass Books, 2013), 19.

3. Ricketson, *Follower First*, 39.

4. Armstrong, *Followership*, 77.

5. Sweet, *I Am a Follower*, 164.

6. Collins with Cooley, *Creative Followership*, 19.

7. Fred Smith, "Does He or She Have the Gift of Leadership?" *Building Church Leaders*, Accessed Dec 21, 2012, http://www.buildingchurchleaders.com/assessments/individuals/doesheorshehavethegiftofleadership.html.

8. Ricketson, *Follower First*, 48; with my personal paraphrases.

9. Collins with Cooley, *Creative Followership*, 15.

10. Robert Kelley, in *The Power of Followership*, chap. 3, presents an excellent paradigm for considering why various people become a follower. Included are categories such as those looking to be mentored, discipled, or apprenticed as well as those who are comrades and loyalists, all of which contain an element of specific attachment to a particular person as leader.

11. Chaleff, *The Courageous Follower*, 13.

12. Imoukhuede, *Discovering Followership*, 15.

Chapter 4: Leadership According to Followers

1. Michael Useem paints a compelling picture of this "translating" role of followers in his book *Leading Up*, chap. 8.

2. Collins with Cooley, *Creative Followership*, 61.

3. Will Smale, "Tommy Ahlers: The software boss who says he was born to lead," *BBC News*, December 2, 2013, http://www.bbc.co.uk/news/business-25085677.

4. Larry Hirschhorn, *Reworking Authority* (Cambridge, MA: MIT Press), 68.

Chapter 5: Obligations of Followership

1. Hirschhorn, *Reworking Authority*, 84.

2. Ira Chaleff's book, *The Courageous Follower*, contains extensive perspective on when and how followers may find themselves needing to take morally prompted action.

3. Collins with Cooley, *Creative Followership*, 100.

4. Kellerman, *Followership*, 66.

5. Kellerman, *Followership*, 254.

6. I am indebted to Rusty Ricketson (*Follower First*, 11, 100) and Leonard Sweet (*I Am a Follower*, 21) for surfacing this notion of crisis of followership.

7. Kelley, *The Power of Followership*, 34.

8. Imoukhuede, *Discovering Followership*, 80.

9. Ira Chaleff, "2014 Leadership Conference of the U.S. Naval Academy, January 27–29, 2014. Panel Discussion 2." Accessed July 3, 2014. https://www.youtube.com/watch?v=hBJ7LQVONSc.

10. Useem, *Leading Up*, 3.

11. Useem, *Leading Up*, 255.

12. See, for example, Useem, *Leading Up*, 209.

13. Cross-cultural differences may also come into play here, as different cultures expect follower input or permit followers to provide correction to varying degrees. Chapter 10 has more information about cross-cultural factors relevant to engaging in healthy, appropriate, and communicative relationships with your leaders.

14. Chaleff, *The Courageous Follower*, 29.

15. Chaleff, *The Courageous Follower*, 220.

16. Collins with Cooley, *Creative Followership*, 65.

17. Ricketson, *Follower First*, 125.

18. Chaleff, *The Courageous Follower*, 98.

19. T. J. MacLeslie, *Designed for Relationship* (Seattle: Parvaim, 2013), lays out this paradigm of five circles of our humanity, addressing each as critical for our health and wholeness. It is a recommended resource for personal growth and for encouraging the growth of others.

20. Sweet, *I Am a Follower*, 34.

21. Imoukhuede, *Discovering Followership*, 5, 86.

22. Kelley, *The Power of Followership*, 146.

Chapter 6: Contributions of Followership

1. Ricketson, *Follower First*, 59.

2. Gene Edwards, *A Tale of Three Kings* (Carol Stream, IL: Tyndale Hourse), chap. 25.

3. Kellerman, *Followership*, 9.

4. Chaleff, *The Courageous Follower*, xix.

5. Useem, *Leading Up*, 1.

6. Rob Goffee and Gareth Jones, *Authentic Followership* (Boston: Harvard Business School Press, 2007), 12.

7. Chaleff, *The Courageous Follower*, 134.

8. Collins with Cooley, *Creative Followership*, 110.

Chapter 7: Ownership: Passion in Action

1. Jef Williams, *Leadership-Followership 360 °* (O'Fallon, IL: JefWilCo Publishing, 2011), 27.

2. Robert Kelley, *How to Be a Star at Work* (New York: Three Rivers Press, 1999), 33.

3. From the New Testament, Peter following Jesus was yet another example of the same two tendencies.

Chapter 9: Relational Challenges to Following Well

1. Hirschhorn, *Reworking Authority*, 89.

Chapter 10: Cultural Challenges to Following Well

1. David C. Thomas and Kerr Inkson. *Cultural Intelligence: Living and Working Globally* (San Francisco: Berrett-Koehler, 2009), 15.

2. See his various books, including *Cultures and Organizations* (New York: HarperCollins, 1994), as well as his website: http://geert-hofstede.com/dimensions.html. In addition to power distance (likened to "concentration of authority"), uncertainty avoidance is the other primary cultural characteristic that Hofstede identifies as significantly affecting our thinking about organizations. For those interested in this material and in exploring more of the application of Hofstede's paradigm to organizational structures, I recommend reading further on his website as well as chapter 6 of *Cultures and Organizations*.

3. Hofstede, *Cultures and Organizations*, 15.

4. Hofstede, *Cultures and Organizations*, 24.

5. Hofstede, *Cultures and Organizations*, 36.

6. Hofstede, *Cultures and Organizations*, 45.

7. See Hofstede, *Cultures and Organizations*, 116, 126.

8. Chaleff, *The Courageous Follower*, 181–83.

9. Hirschhorn, *Reworking Authority*, 128.

10. Thomas and Inkson, *Cultural Intelligence*, 8.

11. Thomas and Inkson, *Cultural Intelligence*, 12.

12. "How Many People Groups Are There?" on The Joshua Project website, accessed January 14, 2014. http://www.joshuaproject.net/how-many-people-groups.php (page discontinued).

13. Thomas and Inkson, *Cultural Intelligence*, 33.

14. Hofstede, *Cultures and Organizations*, 140.

15. I recommend chapter 3 of Hofstede's *Cultures and Organizations* for an in-depth exploration of the individual-collectivist dimension of culture.

16. Thomas and Inkson, *Cultural Intelligence*, 33.

17. Hofstede, *Cultures and Organizations*, 50.

18. Thomas and Inkson, *Cultural Intelligence*, 14.

19. Hofstede, *Cultures and Organizations*, 5.

20. Thomas and Inkson, *Cultural Intelligence*, 72.

21. Thomas and Inkson, *Cultural Intelligence*, 71.

22. Hofstede, *Cultures and Organizations*, 13.

Chapter 11: Resources for Personal Development

1. Thomas and Inkson, *Cultural Intelligence*, 16.

2. Thomas and Inkson, *Cultural Intelligence*, 54.

3. These four questions are trademarked by the ClarionModel.

4. "The angel and the monster: Mother Teresa and Lady Gaga are the latest icons of the leadership industry. Don't laugh," *The Economist* (June 2, 2011). Also available online at http://www.economist.com/node/18772204.

5. Bobby Clinton's constellation model of mentoring (also referred to as the mentoring matrix) is a helpful description of these various spheres of mentoring relationships. His mentor reader (available for purchase at http://bobbyclinton.com/store/readers/mentor-reader/) contains an article summarizing this model (pages 19–22).

6. For more resources, check out: http://www.kwintessential.co.uk/resources/country-profiles.html   or   http://geert-hofstede.com/countries.html.

Chapter 12: Clarifying Vision and Role

1. Kelley, *The Power of Followership*, 132.

2. Kelley, *The Power of Followership*, 134, 138.

3. Hofstede, *Cultures and Organizations*, 124.

4. Hofstede, *Cultures and Organizations*, 125.

5. Hofstede, *Cultures and Orgins*, 153.

6. Thomas and Inkson, *Cultural Intelligence*, 110.

7. Ricketson, *Follower First*, 60.

Chapter 13: Rest as a Resource

1. Stephen Covey, *First Things First*, abridged audiotape, 1999. Quoted in James Lawrence, *Growing Leaders*, (Peabody, MA: Hendrickson), 71.

2. I see this aspect also contained in the commandment related to Sabbath, as the instruction also stipulates, "six days shall you labor and do all your work, but the seventh day is a sabbath ... " (Deut 5:13-14a, NASB).

3. This perspective is not too dissimilar from the observations made by Hofstede of the cultural influence on our view toward work. Some cultures will embrace an ethos of "live in order to work" while others display a value on "work in order to live." See Hofstede, *Cultures and Organizations*, 93.

4. This too is an idea captured in the Sabbath commandment, which also relates that a foundation for engaging in the time of ceasing and rest was for the Hebrew people to remember that they had once been enslaved—as human production machines—but no longer. As such, their lives were no longer only about doing, but could be more about being: being healthy, being free, being in relationship with each other, and being in relationship with God. See Deuteronomy 5:15.

Chapter 14: The Leader–Follower Dynamic

1. Kellerman, *Followership*, xx.

2. Kelley, *The Power of Followership*, 160.

3. Kellerman, *Followership*, 64.

4. Gene Boccialetti, *It Takes Two* (San Francisco: Jossey-Bass, 1995), 3; emphasis original.

5. Boccialetti, *It Takes Two*, 2, 156.

6. Boccialetti, *It Takes Two*, 48.

7. Chaleff, *The Courageous Follower*, 12.

8. Boccialetti, *It Takes Two*, 99.

9. Boccialetti, *It Takes Two*, 139.

Chapter 15: Communication and Trust

1. Imoukhuede, *Discovering*, 73.

2. Hofstede, *Cultures and Organizations*, 217.

3. Ricketson, *Follower First*, 9.

4. Ricketson, *Follower First*, 67.

5. Collins with Cooley, *Creative Followership*, 121.

6. Armstrong, *Followership*, 187.

7. Chaleff, *The Courageous Follower*, 81.

8. Chaleff, *The Courageous Follower*, 164; emphasis original.

9. Boccialetti, *It Takes Two*, 52.

10. Boccialetti, *It Takes Two*, 108.

Chapter 16: Cooperation and Pre-Forgiveness

1. Boccialetti, *It Takes Two*, 149; emphasis mine.

2. Kent Bjugstad, et al., "A Fresh Look at Followership: A Model for Matching Followership and Leadership Styles," *Journal of Behavioral and Applied Management* 7, no 3 (2006): 307.

3. Hirschhorn, *Reworking Authority*, 8.

Chapter 17: Influence, Submission, and Reward

1. Boccialetti, *It Takes Two*, 22.

2. Kelley, *How to Be a Star at Work*, 160.

3. Collins with Cooley, *Creative Followership*, 31.

4. Collins with Cooley, *Creative Followership*, 65.

5. Boccialetti, *It Takes Two*, 74.

6. Boccialetti, *It Takes Two*, 170.

7. David Staal, "Influence Those Above You," MS Word document available at *Building Church Leaders*. http://www.buildingchurchleaders.com/downloads/childrensministry/influencethoseaboveyou/

8. Ricketson, *Follower First* , 111.

Chapter 18: What the Relationship Can Achieve

1. Chaleff, *The Courageous Follower*, 1.

Chapter 19: Following "Poor" Leaders

1. James C. Galvin, *I've Got Your Back* (Elgin, IL: Tenth Power Publishing, 2012), 99.

2. Kellerman, *Followership*, 233.

3. See Kellerman, *Followership*, 230.

4. Galvin, *I've Got Your Back*, 48.

5. Chaleff, *The Courageous Follower*, 165.

6. Armstrong, *Followership*, 78.

7. Chaleff, *The Courageous Follower*, 133.

8. Galvin, *I've Got Your Back*, 50.

9. Collins with Cooley, *Creative Followership*, 27.

Chapter 21: Peer Relationships

1. Chaleff, *The Courageous Follower*, 32.

2. Thomas and Inkson, *Cultural Intelligence*, 135.

Chapter 22: Informal Leadership

1. See Kelley, *How to be a Star at Work*, chap. 10.

2. Kelley, *How to be a Star at Work*, 176.

3. Armstrong, *Followership*, 57.

4. Kelley, *How to be a Star at Work*, 182.

5. Kelley, *How to be a Star at Work*, 177.

6. Useem, *Leading Up*, 276.

Chapter 23: A Perspective on Leadership

1. Galvin, *I've Got Your Back*, 110, 194.

2. Dennis L. Gorton with Tom Allen, *Leading the Followers by Following the Leader* (Camp Hill, PA: Christian Publications, 2000), 24.

3. Kelley, *The Power of Followership*, 229.

4. Galvin, *I've Got Your Back*, 61.

5. Joanna E. Sears, "Followership Experiences as a Catalyst for Leadership Development: A Qualitative Study," 2.

6. Williams, *Leadership-Followership*, 29.

7. Hofstede, *Cultures and Organizations*, 28.

8. Williams, *Leadership-Followership*, 32.

Chapter 24: Displaying Dependence

1. Hirschhorn, *Reworking Authority*, 18.

2. It is popular to speak of situational leadership, adapting one's leadership style to particular circumstances. I appreciate Thomas and Inkson's encouragement toward cross-cultural situational leadership: "A culturally intelligent leader is able to find a leadership style that strikes a balance between his or her preferred (normal) style, the expectations of followers, and the demands of the situation ... . Understanding the expectations that followers have of their leaders is a key element in a culturally intelligent approach to leadership" (*Cultural Intelligence*, 127).

Chapter 25: Establishing the Environment

1. The four-phase model of stages of group development put forth by Bruce Tuckman in 1965 is extremely useful; it provides encouragement about the challenges and possibilities that groups experience as they figure out how to work together. The four stages are forming, storming, norming, and performing. The storming stage is an especially signif-icant one for teams to engage in so that they can emerge into a new place of healthy norms.

2. Sweet, *I Am a Follower*, 177.

3. Ricketson, *Follower First*, 73.

4. Hirschhorn, *Reworking Authority*, 21.

5. Thomas and Inkson, *Cultural Intelligence*, 112.

6. Thomas and Inkson, *Cultural Intelligence*, 142.

7. Gorton with Allen, *Leading the Followers*, 46.

Chapter 27: Empowering and Promoting

1. Boccialetti, *It Takes Two*, 137.

2. Patrick Lencioni, *The Five Dysfunctions of a Team* (San Francisco: Jossey-Bass, 2002), 74.

3. Kelley, *The Power of Followership*, 228.

Final Thoughts

1. Kellerman, *Followership*, 257.

2. Imoukhuede, *Discovering Followership*, 99.

3. Boccialetti, *It Takes Two*, 170.

4. Collins with Cooley, *Creative Followership*, 79.

5. Ricketson, *Follower First*, 142.

6. You can find the full text and an audio recording of this story online at http://etc.usf.edu/lit2go/79/just-so-stories/1296/the-cat-that-walked-by-himself/.

SUBJECT AND AUTHOR INDEX